Complicity in Discourse and Practice

It is commonplace to say that we are living in troubled times. Liberal democracy is in crisis. Academic freedom is seriously constrained. The media offers less insight and analysis than could be expected given the proliferation of communication tools. Based on decades of research into the social and ideological functioning of discourse and with a focus on politics, universities, and the media, Jef Verschueren offers an analysis of current practices, asks whether we are all complicit, and makes suggestions for what we can do.

Central to this book is the notion of derailed reflexivity, referring to the observation that politics, institutions, and news reporting tend to be excessively aimed at public opinion, impression management, and clicks, to the detriment of policies addressing social justice issues, high-quality service, and media content. Highlighting that education is the cornerstone for democratic choices and ensures that we can critically assess media content, this book shows that shared responsibility can be a source of hope and that everyone has the power to intervene.

Complicity in Discourse and Practice is a call to action for readers and a plea for actively minding the ecology of the public sphere.

Jef Verschueren is Emeritus Professor of Linguistics at the University of Antwerp and Secretary General of the International Pragmatics Association

Routledge Focus on Applied Linguistics

Making Sense of the Intercultural
Finding DeCentred Threads
Adrian Holliday and Sara Amadasi

Mobile Assisted Language Learning Across Educational Contexts
Edited by Valentina Morgana and Agnes Kukulska-Hulme

Complicity in Discourse and Practice
Jef Verschueren

For more information about this series, please visit: www.routledge.com/
Routledge-Focus-on-Applied-Linguistics/book-series/RFAL

Complicity in Discourse and Practice

Jef Verschueren

Routledge
Taylor & Francis Group

LONDON AND NEW YORK

First published 2022
by Routledge
2 Park Square, Milton Park, Abingdon, Oxon OX14 4RN

and by Routledge
605 Third Avenue, New York, NY 10158

Routledge is an imprint of the Taylor & Francis Group, an informa business

© 2022 Jef Verschueren

British Library Cataloguing-in-Publication Data
A catalogue record for this book is available from the British Library

Library of Congress Cataloging-in-Publication Data
Names: Verschueren, Jef, author.
Title: Complicity in discourse and practice / Jef Verschueren.
Description: London; New York: Routledge, 2021. | Series: Routledge focus on applied linguistics | Includes bibliographical references and index. | Contents: In society – At the university – Through the media – Recap: sharing responsibility – Prospect: An ecology of the public sphere? | Summary: "Complicity in Discourse and Practice is a call to action for readers and a plea for actively minding the ecology of the public sphere" – Provided by publisher.
Identifiers: LCCN 2021014506 | ISBN 9781032072876 (hardback) | ISBN 9781032072883 (paperback) | ISBN 9781003206354 (ebook)
Subjects: LCSH: Rhetoric–Political aspects. | Responsibility. | Mass media–Political aspects. | Mass media and public opinion. | Communication in politics. | Discourse analysis–Politcal aspects. | Language and culture.
Classification: LCC P301.5.P67 V47 2021 | DDC 401/.41–dc23
LC record available at https://lccn.loc.gov/2021014506

ISBN: 9781032072876 (hbk)
ISBN: 9781032072883 (pbk)
ISBN: 9781003206354 (ebk)

DOI: 10.4324/9781003206354

Typeset in Times New Roman
by Deanta Global Publishing Services, Chennai, India

"But in our time, as in every time,
the impossible is the least one can demand."

James Baldwin (1963, p. 104)

For Jacob, Rebecca, Alexandra
the future

Contents

Acknowledgments

When growing up in post-war Europe in the 1950s and 1960s, our world was rife with palpable problems. Cities and economies had to be rebuilt, fractured societies healed. Luxury was reserved for the happy few. Radio and television brought distant wars and rebellions into every home. Colonies were struggling (often fighting, literally) for independence. And the nuclear arms race introduced the dubious safety of mutually assured destruction, undeniable MADness. Yet, I remember a great deal of optimism. We felt that we could make the world a better place.

No doubt, a lot of progress has been made. My generation can boast achievements that would have been hard to imagine. But we have also failed inexcusably. Despite unparalleled economic growth, despite the technical skills needed to turn natural resources into an acceptable standard of living for everyone alive today, that is not exactly the outcome we have produced. Despite unprecedented ease of communication, what we get to know about the world is pitifully fragmented and profoundly polluted, and strife and conflict overshadow dialogue. Despite clever statisticians' calculations that, overall, the world has become more peaceful, deadly violence is rampant. On top of all that, our living environment is getting seriously damaged. Perhaps most seriously of all, the realm of politics, where we should find the necessary levers for change, is not in good shape, to say the least.

Merely nestling at a cynical distance, however, is not an option. We have not reached the point of gloom where only hopelessness would beckon. More equality, dialogue, peace, and even decent democratic politics are still entirely possible. The following pages are an attempt to find a realistic renewal of erstwhile optimism, even if what they describe looks grim. My tool will be a bird's-eye view of *practices* – inevitably couched in *discourse* – in areas of public life I have engaged in as a scholar: Politics in the face of diversity, higher education (exemplifying a type of neoliberal institutional context shared by many working adults across sectors of professional activity), and the media.

x *Acknowledgments*

This essay has been brewing for a decade. It was first conceived during a year of residence in Paris, as a guest of the *École des hautes études en sciences sociales* (EHESS) at the *Maison des Sciences de l'Homme*. This stimulating and peaceful retreat followed eight hectic years as Dean of the Faculty of Arts at the University of Antwerp. Busy professional lives offer little space for careful reflection. There is always a new and urgent matter to take care of. After a while, you can no longer avoid the feeling that you are losing sight of the essentials. One of these essentials, for me, was the engagement in societal debate, which I had participated in more vigorously in the final decade of the last century. Meanwhile, however, so much had been happening that it was not just a matter of picking up where I had left off. I took my time. Until the COVID-19 semi-lockdown of early 2020 forced me to sit down, trying to formulate what I had been thinking of and jotting down along the way.

I cannot even begin to express my gratitude to all the people, friends and family, colleagues and students, at home and abroad, who have had a formative influence on the ideas and sentiments expressed in the following pages. Enumerating some would do injustice to others. Somewhere in this essay I say, "people tend not to be so terribly original." People close to me professionally and personally will recognize a lot of themselves in what I write. I hope there will also be a hint of recognition for you, the reader, so that you can use some of my reflections as sources of inspiration for thinking about (if not coping with) these troubled times. Troubled they are, in many ways. But let me not get ahead of my story and acknowledge some people's direct contributions instead.

In addition to a very helpful anonymous reviewer, I am seriously indebted to Andrew Carlin, Helmut Gruber, Jens Maesse, Michael Meeuwis, Todd Nicewonger, Jan-Ola Östman, Ben Rampton, Paul Verhaeghe, Ann Verhaert, Rod Watson, and Jan Zienkowski, who all saw an earlier draft of this text. Some of them provided extensive comments. Others made just a few pertinent remarks. Together they offered so many useful suggestions that I cannot possibly identify them as I go along. So, I must plead guilty to plagiarizing at least some formulations; I also read up on work that I was told to have a look at; and I followed advice that makes the current version hard to recognize, probably even for them. All remaining errors and infelicities remain my own. Thanks are also due to Routledge editor Nadia Seemungal-Owen, who believed in this project from the start.

If you are familiar with my academic work on language use and discourse, you know that I tend to link research to social issues. In this essay, I deliberately let political, social, institutional, and media-related preoccupations take the lead. You will not find in-depth analysis of discourse data. Yet I hope the academic foundations of my observations and arguments still shine through, as the issues to be dealt with are invariably anchored in a world of discourse. Familiarity with the underlying technicalities for analysis, however, is not presupposed. You will also be able to follow my account as an interested reader coming from completely different fields. Writing this text is a modest way of trying to give something back to a wider society, the benefits of which I have been allowed to enjoy – a fact that I gratefully acknowledge.

Prologue

Indignation, perhaps anger, may have been your most conspicuous sentiment for a while. If it was, it was well nourished. How it was nourished depends on who you are, and where you were when.

When – over a decade ago now – the banking system was on the verge of collapse under the weight of megalomaniacal speculations in a virtual financial world, your anger may have been aroused by the thought that taxes on honest and productive labor were poured into the sinkholes of modern capitalism. Or you may have directly suffered the terrifying consequences of being thrust into substandard living conditions, losing home or livelihood.

When terror struck, killing and maiming in what seemed like peaceful surroundings, you may have been irate about so much madness. Or you may have felt the injustice of selective indignation immune to the incessant horror befalling distant others, in parts of the world torn by war.

You may also have watched in disbelief how easily short-term economic and political goals feed the denial of environmental risks. Or how unprepared the champions of the free market's invisible-hand efficiency are when a global pandemic strikes, leaving national or local authorities to scramble for shelter.

You have seen *Indignados*, the *Occupy* movements, *les gilets jaunes* – the yellow vests – and *Black Lives Matter* or *Extinction Rebellion*. These are only some of the most mediatized expressions of indignation that have passed our way. Like me, you probably did not paint them all with the same brush.

Less ostensive but pervasive struggles for political freedom, for basic rights to safety, shelter, food, education, and health care, may have been a more ephemeral presence in your mind. But clearly, fully justified indignation has earned its place in the fight against inequality, exploitation, dire misery, structural discrimination, or the utter neglect of the world we live in.

Indignation, of course, has its targets, the bearers of responsibility. But *between indignation and responsibility, there is a world of complicity.*

This essay embraces hope. But hope without action is vain. Action may require pointing a finger at others. Assigning responsibility may be what we need to do. But not until we ascribe a share of responsibility to ourselves, can we also *take responsibility* and act accordingly. In a complex world, in the absence of pure black and white, we must therefore explore where complicity starts, for you and for me, and how far it goes. *Recognizing complicity may give us unexpected power.* It may snap us out of helpless inaction and sterile blaming. It is an antidote to cynical resignation to all the forces that trigger indignation. It may also bridge the gap between opposing poles, as guilt and innocence – without losing their relevance – become more fluid.

The perspective I am taking can only be my own: As member of a society that is historically situated at the beginning of the third millennium and geographically in a prosperous and highly autonomous region of a small European Union member state; as a person with a working-class background, but who spent his entire professional life in the sheltered realm of universities; as a media consumer trying to stay informed and understand some of what happens in the world beyond my personal experience. This positioning defines the structure of this essay: *One* – "in society"; *two* – "at the university" (merely exemplifying the wider field of education and institutional contexts in general); and *three* – "through the media."

You may not share many of the particulars with me. But you are contemporary, and no matter where you live, the current order of the globe ensures connections, somehow. You have also been touched by education, even if, unlike me, you have moved on from school or university, in which case you may have encountered different institutional settings comparable in various ways. And like for me, most of what you know or think about the world is filtered through a maze of media.

My personal perspective is not only shaped by social background, education, and media consumption. Nor is it exclusively based on research in my areas of expertise, language use and discourse. It also incorporates convictions with a clear political label. You will soon see that I belong to an old-school political left wing. If that is not your corner of the woods, you may fundamentally disagree with some of my analyses. You may even be offended by my occasional refusal to mince my words. Your attribution of responsibility may be different from mine. Your indignation and anger may be directed precisely at most of what I stand for.

Yet, I invite you to join me in this exploration. You may decide that you do not want to assume the role of fellow traveler. There is no need. Being an observer or partner in dialogue may be just as relevant. Even – maybe especially – if you think we live in the best of all possible worlds.

1   In society

We dive in at the deep end, the divisive side of society and its violent excesses, acts and events which I trust you would be unwilling to be associated with. This is a most confrontational testing ground for the notion of complicity. So, please bear with me along the first disturbing pages of this essay, as they are not without significance.

Terror and complicity

22 July 2011. A low-profile native of an affluent Northern European country detonates a home-made fertilizer bomb in the capital's government district. Eight people killed. Not much later, he hunts down camping socialist youngsters on an idyllic island. In cold blood, he shoots 69 of them to death – followed by composed acquiescence to his arrest. You remember the names: Anders Behring Breivik, Oslo, Utøya. Judging from the 1,518-page "compendium" which he had just released through the internet, he found justification for his atrocities in the indirect responsibility of his victims for the Islamization of Europe, the decline of European culture and identity. It was his duty to arrest the decline. His deeds, therefore, were cruel but necessary.

Complicity is the underlying notion serving this cavalier defender of European culture to legitimate the carnage. In his words, by supporting immigration and multiculturalism, "European political elites implement the agendas of our enemies and ignore the interests of their own people" (p. 599). He continues, "They are thus collaborators and traitors and should be treated accordingly." His targets, the individuals as well as the institutions they associated themselves with, did not have to be Islamic. They were to blame for their acquiescence to, or applause for, diversity. They failed to oppose and sometimes encouraged the unacceptable. They were complicit, hence guilty.

DOI: 10.4324/9781003206354-1

You may also remember that complicity with Breivik's acts of terror – in the form of support for some of the ideas that prompted him into action – was at the heart of a debate that flared up briefly. It was triggered, first, by some far-right politicians expressing sympathy for the ideology that prompted Breivik into action, notwithstanding their agreement with the public condemnation of the massacre itself. Second, a quick screening of the "compendium" showed striking similarities with widely shared and accepted ideas circulating in the extreme right corners of society. Breivik even named some well-known politicians as sources of inspiration or in support of his points of view. The progressive left in Europe saw an opportunity to point out the dangers of a nationalist ideology, and so they did.

The controversy was short-lived. Politicians who openly sympathized with Breivik were reprimanded and sometimes expelled by their parties. And the argument was made, not without reason, that blaming all believers in a world view for the terror caused by extremists in its name, would be comparable to confusing the bombing of a family planning clinic with run-of-the-mill pro-life activism, or equating ecologically inspired sabotage, the so-called eco-terrorism, with strong ecological convictions.

Perhaps you are convinced that only the perpetrators of heinous acts, and those consciously involved in their planning, can be held responsible for them. Direct responsibility, or legal and moral accountability for specific acts, tends to be associated with deliberation and intentionality; what is done is done "on purpose." Assigning responsibility would be easy if we could invoke a simple concept of law. But with laws as unambiguous rules, there would be no need for lawyers. As Hart reminded us a long time ago, "in the vast majority of cases that trouble the courts, neither statutes nor precedents in which the rules are allegedly contained allow of only one result." He continues: "The judge has to choose between alternative meanings to be given to the words of a statute or between rival interpretations of what a precedent 'amounts to'" (Hart 1994, p. 12).

To the misleading simplicity of legal accountability, we must add distant forms of responsibility and multiple shades of complicity. We cannot avoid doing so in a complex world, full of categories of events with blurry boundaries. It may help to continue where we started, with the category of "terrorism." History provides us with a long list of destructive and often murderous acts for which we can probably agree that they somehow involve "guilt," that someone "is to blame."

But history does not make things easy. Perpetrators come in different guises. They operate in different realms. Their motivations as well as their modes of operation vary – also over time. The range of iniquitous effects of their actions often defies sensible comparison. The combined assessment of motivations and effects, depending on the stance we take, opens a kaleidoscope of incommensurable evaluations, from understanding and sympathy to outright condemnation.

The Global Terrorism Database[1] lists over 150,000 incidents categorized as "terrorist" from 1970 to 2015 – that is, an average of more than nine on every single day over a 45-year period. You can probably name only a few of those, imprinted in our collective memory by massive media coverage.

If you are the right age, you may remember the bombing campaign (with high-profile targets such as the US Capitol, the Pentagon, the US Department of State) by the Weather Underground, a militant left-wing organization opposing, amongst other things, the Vietnam War, in the early 1970s. Their advance warnings prevented casualties – except for three of their own. More deadly revolutionary movements operating throughout the second half of the 20th century included the Irish Republican Army (IRA) and *Euskadi Ta Askatusuna* (ETA, "Basque Country and Freedom"). With roots in the 19th century, the IRA metamorphosed on several occasions, while preserving the legacy of resistance against British imperialism. ETA rose against Franco's dictatorship in Spain but persisted in the struggle for Basque self-determination after the transition into democracy. Both may have ceased violent action, but not until ETA had been responsible, since 1968, for over 800 killings, thousands of injuries, and dozens of abductions, while the Northern Irish "Troubles" from 1969 to 1998 cost over 3,500 lives (roughly 60% at the hands of IRA-related republicans, 30% attributed to loyalist paramilitary groups, and 10% to British security forces). The majority of those killed were civilians. A less advertised movement, similar in spirit, that may have escaped your attention, was the separatist and leftist *Front du libération du Québec* which, between 1963 and 1970, in seemingly tranquil Canada, was involved in 160 violent incidents, leaving eight people dead and many more injured.

Flirting with the boundaries of legitimate warfare, "liberation" has served as the great motivator on many occasions. Liberation from dictatorship was the shared goal of the *Tupamaros* in Uruguay and the *Vanguarda Armada Revolucionária Palmares* in Brazil, both left-wing organizations. Operating in the 1960s and early 1970s, the former did not shy away from assassinations, while the latter's major feats were robberies. The Uruguayan and Brazilian dictatorships both ended in 1985. Later, José Mujica, erstwhile combative member of the *Tupamaros* (for which he spent a total of 13 years in prison, to be released under the 1985 amnesty law), served as the 40th President of Uruguay from 2010 to 2015. Former *VAR Palmares* member Dilma Roussef (probably without any major role in the organization) became the 36th President of Brazil from 2011 to 2016. Clearly, transgression, crime, guilt, and responsibility are not stable historical categories.

Liberation from occupation rather than dictatorship was the goal of the Palestine Liberation Organization (PLO), serving as an umbrella for organizations such as *Fatah* (its most prominent "member") and the left-wing Popular Front for the Liberation of Palestine (PFLP). Under the PLO umbrella, aircraft hijacking developed into a fine art in the 1960s and 1970s (with as many as four in one day on 6 September 1970), and violence aimed at Israeli civilians as well as military personnel made numerous casualties. Under PLO leadership, Palestine has achieved its present status as a "Non-member Observer State" at the United Nations since 2012. Yet it does not look like the struggle has reached its conclusion. There is a continued tug-of-war over the definition of Palestinian political violence as a form of resistance or of terrorism. Again, history will decide. Having said that, the exertion of power will be involved, so that responsibility must inevitably be shared by the powerful agents who will help to decide the outcome – not just by people on the ground.

A comparable history, with a more desirable outcome than the currently unresolved two-state solution for the Israeli-Palestinian conflict, can be sketched for Nelson Mandela's African National Congress. The ANC was founded in 1912 as an anti-apartheid opposition party, banned in 1960, continuing as an underground guerilla and sabotage network, lifted to political legitimacy again in 1990 to become South Africa's leading political family. But it was not taken off the US terror watch list until 2008.

Recent acts in the name of independence must be easy to recall. Think of the three-day school siege (starting 1 September 2004) in Beslan, a town in the Russian Caucasus, where the fight for an independent Chechnya left nearly 400 people dead. Earlier Chechen actions had led to the death of at least 140 people when they attacked the southern Russian town of Budyonnovsk in 1995 and took hostages in the local hospital, and of 170 people in a Moscow theater in 2002. It is impossible to condone murder. But if legitimate grievances are at issue, are the killers the only ones responsible?

Racially motivated property destruction, violence, and random killings are still the order of the day. You know the white-supremacist Ku Klux Klan, still in existence today, though with greatly diminished membership. Their trademark activities were bombings and burnings of black schools and churches (at least one as recent as 1995). The years of the civil rights movement also saw violence against and assassinations of black and white activists. Former KKK Imperial Wizard David Duke, a member of the US House of Representatives from 1989 to 1992, is still politically active, openly antisemitic, and he applauded Donald Trump's campaign attacks on immigrants and Muslims. Is it a whim of our imagination to see a link between the violence and the political rhetoric, even if we cannot lay blame for one on the other?

Less well-known is the far-right extremism of the Jewish Defense League, established in 1968 by Rabbi Meir Kahane to counter antisemitism, and responsible for several assassinations of prominent Arab Americans in the ensuing decades. A notorious US member of the League was Baruch Goldstein, the perpetrator of the Hebron massacre on 25 February 1994, a shooting in the Ibrahimi Mosque at the Cave of the Patriarchs compound, killing 29 Palestinians and wounding another 125. Was this an individual's hatred, or the morbid outgrowth of legitimate resistance to racism turned racist?

Still in the realm of racially motivated violence, you may have entirely forgotten the so-called Zebra murders which paralyzed the San Francisco Bay Area from October 1973 to April 1974, with mostly white victims, and committed by a group of African Americans calling themselves "Death Angels." Amongst other things, they practiced the art of drive-by shootings. They did not have a monopoly on this method of sowing terror. Nor, unfortunately, are such incidents confined to a relatively distant past. In fact, they are so frequent and random that it is impossible to categorize them in any sensible way. A recent survey identified 733 drive-by shooting incidents in the US in a six-month period from July through December 2008, killing 154 and injuring 631 – with the state of California leading in the ranking with 148 incidents, 40 lethal victims, and 129 injured.[2]

In Europe, throughout the final decades of the 20th century, extreme left and extreme right were outbidding each other in the quest for public attention. In Germany, a group of leftist youngsters engaged in violent action. They found justification, amongst other things, in the continued position of privilege and power enjoyed by former Nazis; they felt they had to make up for the resistance which their parents had failed to put up before and during World War II. You are right, I am thinking of the *Rote Armee Fraktion* or Baader-Meinhof group. Roughly 300 attacks, at least 34 dead. Their Italian counterpart, the *Brigate Rosse* (with a 21st-century pendant in the *Partito Comunista Politico-Militare*), was a left-wing paramilitary organization responsible for robberies, kidnappings, and assassinations (including the murder of Prime Minister Aldo Moro in 1978 – an event that also cost the lives of five people in Moro's entourage when he was abducted). They were not the only ones contributing to the "years of lead" (*Anni di piombo*). In four years, from 1977 to 1981, 33 murders were committed by the neofascist *Nuclei Armati Rivoluzionari* (NAR), an organization to which also the 1980 bombing of the Bologna train station (85 killed, 188 wounded) was attributed.

Africa and Asia have had their share of terrorist violence. A recent but superficial scan of Africa takes us from the Algiers bombings in the north (11

April 2007), hitting the headquarters of the prime minister and a police station, killing 23 and injuring 162, via sprees of violence in northeastern Nigeria (the arena of Boko Haram) and the Democratic Republic of the Congo (with 268 incidents and 877 terror victims in a five-year period – not counting the innumerable victims of civil war), to post-apartheid South Africa, where often unclaimed but clearly politically inspired violent attacks are still rampant.

Asia is offering a sad spectacle. Looking from Europe, it starts in Syria, Iraq, Afghanistan, and Pakistan, all with countless cases of deadly violence. It continues via India with, for instance, the series of coordinated shootings and bombings that held Mumbai in its grip for four days in November 2008, leaving 164 people dead and over 300 wounded. We get all the way into China, where on 18 September 2015, at least 50 were killed when people armed with knives attacked the Sogan Colliery coal mine in the Xinjiang region. The attack was attributed to Uighur separatism which is held responsible for an underpublicized but long string of lethal actions. Even Japan has its so-called Revolutionary Army, regularly targeting US Army bases on Japanese soil.

Obviously, this is only a brief anthology of events overshadowed in current public consciousness by 9/11 (11 September 2001, attacks on the New York World Trade Center towers and the Pentagon); 11-M (11 March 2004, the Madrid train bombings); 7/7 (7 July 2005, the London metro and bus bombings); the bomb that killed 224 people on a Russian passenger plane over the Sinai desert on 31 October 2015; the series of coordinated attacks in Paris on 13 November 2015; the suicide attacks on Brussels airport and a Brussels metro station on 22 March 2016; or the truck attacks in Nice on 14 July 2016, in Berlin on 19 December 2016, and in Stockholm on 7 April 2017. All of these are grouped under the label of "Islamic terror," whether at the hands of Al Qaeda, Islamic State, or any of their home-grown operatives.

And then there are all the so-called "lone wolves" – a notion which loses its significance when looking at extended forms of responsibility and complicity, as they are always children of their time and social environment, nourished by powerful belief systems. The names of these notorious individuals you easily remember: Theodore Kaczynski or the Unabomber, the anti-technology anarchist who targeted airline officials and university professors with letter bombs between 1978 and 1995, killing three and injuring 23; or Timothy McVeigh and Terry Nichols, the right-wing sympathizers who killed 168 people and wounded 680 others with a car bomb at a federal government building in Oklahoma City on 19 April 1995. And then, yes, there is Anders Behring Breivik, as well as others he may have inspired, including Brenton Harrison Tarrant who killed 51 people during his mosque shootings in Christchurch, New Zealand, on 15 March 2019.

More easily forgotten are the names of mass murderers whose individual motives remain the object of speculation: Stephen Paddock, who killed 58 and wounded 413 in ten minutes, shooting from his hotel room in Las Vegas on 1 October 2017; Andreas Lubitz, the Germanwings co-pilot who killed 150 people by deliberately crashing flight 9525 from Barcelona to Düsseldorf into the Massif des Trois-Évêchés on 24 March 2015. The list is endless.

This looks like apples and oranges. But I hope you get the message. In the decades before COVID-19 temporarily diverted our attention, public opinion in the Global North developed a spatio-temporally confined fixation with so-called "Islamic" terror. In practice, however, any type of extremism or despair can lead to acts of terror, and so can any type of deep anger based on a sense of injustice, whether justified or not, and the accompanying frustration about unequal access to the means needed to pursue one's goals. Usually, it is a deadly mix of such ingredients. All these incidents belong to a vague category which only has in common that the acts are aimed at making a statement. Sometimes it is purely personal and hard to define. More often, there is a political, religious, or social goal, or a combination of these. Moreover, the statements are meant to have an impact on an audience beyond the direct victims themselves. For violent political action, a further criterion to qualify as terrorism is the transgression of internationally declared (though not necessarily observed) limitations on legitimate warfare, for instance by intentionally targeting non-combatant civilians. As some of the examples have shown, it is here that the boundaries of the category get most easily blurred. For my current purpose, it is not necessary to decide when we are looking at an apple or at an orange. The family resemblance is decisive.

As I already suggested, you may believe that only the perpetrators of heinous acts, and those consciously participating in their planning or execution, can be held directly responsible. But I am sure you have seen the numerous lines of involvement that are evident in most of the (usually deeply political rather than "senseless") violence that has just passed the review. Can one remain convinced, therefore, that everyone else is innocent? Or do we have to start taking considerations in terms of complicity, at various levels, seriously?

Return for a moment to where we started – a treacherously simple case. Legally, and as far as we know, Breivik did not have accomplices. He planned and executed his double attack on his own. But what about the responsibility of the online businesses that provided him with fertilizer for his bomb, or the police uniform he used as cover for crossing onto Utøya? What about the ferry captain who takes him across? What about the people who sold him guns and ammunition? What about the Oslo shooting club where he was practicing? Or what about the designers of World of Warcraft, which he spent a year playing to desensitize himself? They all contributed, in different ways, by enabling Breivik to commit his crimes. But none of them can be held legally accountable. Even if the fertilizer, uniform, and arms sales were illegal, those involved would not be legally responsible for what was done with them, unless they had advance knowledge of Breivik's plans. Also, moral accountability could hardly be claimed for traders of fertilizer, even if rich in ammonium nitrate, and police uniforms, even if fake. For the arms salesmen, a moral charge would imply a condemnation of all dealing in firearms – which you may or may not want to endorse, but which you certainly will not support if you are an American citizen cherishing the Second Amendment. For sure, you would not want to blame the ferry captain, despite his gullible acceptance of Breivik's story that he had been sent over to reassure people on the island after the blast in downtown Oslo.

Clearly, commonplace concepts of guilt, accountability, responsibility, and even complicity, broadly conceived, do not apply. However, direct participation is not the only way of sharing in the guilt for someone else's wrongdoing. You can also do so by commanding, advising, consenting, encouraging, or by not preventing, covering up, being silent, or not denouncing. These are categories of complicity already in use since Thomas Aquinas' 13th-century *Summa Theologica* (cf. Mellema 2016).

Such extended forms of responsibility are commonly invoked to legitimize acts of terror. For Tarrant, his victims simply embodied – without having organized it themselves – "the great replacement" which, in a view shared by many others, endangers Western civilization or can even be interpreted as "white genocide."[3] Breivik ascribed guilt to all his victims for what he saw as the Islamization of Europe. Likewise, in the words of anti-technology anarchist Theodore Kaczynski, "people who willfully and knowingly promote economic growth and technical progress, in our eyes they are criminals, and if they get blown up they deserve it."[4] In a show of good nature he claims to "strongly deplore the kind of indiscriminate slaughter that occurred in the Oklahoma City event" at the hands of Timothy McVeigh, and to be happy, in retrospect, that his own earlier attempt to blow up an aircraft had failed. He even regrets injuring the secretary who opened the bomb package addressed to a computer scientist, his real target. But he does not doubt the overall righteousness in his actions. The victims were guilty, some directly, others by complicity, even if on a gradable scale.

Should you then do a Breivik or Tarrant in reverse, attributing guilt, however indirect, to whoever could be blamed for facilitating their actions?

You may decide that the numerous parties and organizations constituting Europe's radical right share responsibility for Oslo and Utøya. Your reaction may be, with a variegated set of options in between, to fight their ideologies or to bomb their headquarters. The latter, a real Breivik or Tarrant in reverse, probably does not belong to the arsenal of means you are willing to resort to, even if you – like me – are the kind of pacifist who does not believe that violence can always be avoided.

Evaluating the extent of someone's responsibility requires clarity as to what motivates a given instance of complicity, or how, perhaps, it results from putting a praiseworthy goal in the balance against the indirect support for wrongdoing. You will find that such an evaluation is complex. It invites, for one, a discussion of how to avoid paving the road to hell with good intentions. To what extent, for instance, do the relationships which NGOs maintain with governments and the private sector thwart movements for social change and justice by supporting neocolonial capitalist structures, while being devoted to aid and development (cf. Choudry & Kapoor 2013)? Is negotiating with warlords blameworthy if it is the only way to provide humanitarian relief (cf. Lepora & Goodin 2013)? How do we evaluate complicity with evil if war crimes and genocide are enabled by the laudable goal of the United Nations to achieve and preserve peace through absolute non-interventionism (cf. Lebor 2006)? Remember Rwanda 1994 and Srebrenica 1995. Or, returning to the Breivik case, how can you decide to what measure people can be charged with complicity for what he (Breivik) did if they (the potential accomplices) contributed to the general anti-Islamic social and political maelstrom which he used with such ease for justification, while they may perceive themselves as prophets and saviors "just telling the truth" about Islam as a dangerous religion incompatible with Western norms and values?

An evaluation of indirect responsibility also requires clarity as to what position of power and influence the complicit party occupies. The literature on complicity has a strong tendency to situate the issue at the level of individual actors. Even UC Berkeley law professor Christopher Kutz (2000), concerned with the harm brought about by people acting together in what he regards as a "collective age" (an age in which many goals require action by a collection of agents), formulates responsibility for collective action in terms of the accountability of individual participants. Hence his formulation of "The Complicity Principle":

> I am accountable for what others do when I intentionally participate in the wrong they do or harm they cause. I am accountable for the harm or wrong we do together, independent of the actual difference I make.
>
> (Kutz 2000, p. 122)

I will come back later to this formulation of the burden on the shoulders of individuals, irrespective of the actual difference they make.

Ideas, influence, and power

For the time being, I invite you to join me in a different direction.

Underlying blameworthy action, whether collective or individual, there is always a level of ideas that provide the fertile soil for developments that may lead to wrongdoing. Ideas are not the product of individual minds. People tend not to be so terribly original. Ideas spread in a field of societally distributed cognition. We pick them up, or we may reject them. We rarely know where they come from, or what they are based on. But they do have consequences. They form the basis for action.

In that process, there are people with power or influence who can do more than others to determine the directions of ideological development. Typically, they are artists, intellectuals, politicians. Richard Golsan (2006) gives us examples of French writers in the 1940s and 1990s. In the 1940s, Henry de Montherlant, Alphonse de Châteaubriand, and Jean Giono all collaborated, to varying degrees, with the Vichy regime and hence the Nazis. They were apparently led to complicity by blind spots in their thinking which they could (or could not?) have avoided, and which certainly contributed to a general context of acquiescence which facilitated atrocities. Later, in the 1990s, Alain Finkielkraut, Régis Debray, and Stéphane Courtois were all influentially implicated in controversies in which their positions can be seen as contributions to the rise of rightist extremism in Europe: Finkielkraut by his avid support for Tudjman and Croatian independence, in spite of their association with the darker side of Croatian nationalism, the Ustaša movement that embraced Nazism during World War II; Debray with his support for Milosevic, unequivocally casting him as the persecuted party at the time of NATO's (far from irreproachable) attack on Serbia in defense of Kosovo; Courtois by claiming, in a bout of historical revisionism, that the crimes of communism had been far worse than those of Nazism. Between the two periods covered by Golson, relevant reference could be made to Foucault's initial enthusiasm for the Iranian revolution and French intellectuals' support for Maoism in the 1960s.

Restricting my examples to France and turning my attention to the (lack of) acceptance of diversity in Europe, a recent addition should be Renaud Camus' (2011) contribution to the white genocide conspiracy theories of the European extreme right with his writings about "the great replacement."

Combining influence with power, politicians occupy the center stage when it comes to orienting worlds of ideas in relation to social and political processes. You may think of loud-mouthed firebrands such as the UK's Tommy Robinson, co-founder and one-time leader of the English Defence League. They certainly have a role to play in Europe's dominant non-acceptance of diversity, a theme to which I will come back later quite extensively, and which should not be confused with the variable extent to which immigration is legally allowed. Despite their phenomenal influence, their actual political power may remain marginal. That is why – in relation to this topic – a heavier burden of responsibility may rest with mainstream politicians, such as German Chancellor Angela Merkel, former French President Nicolas Sarkozy, and former British Prime Minister David Cameron when they unanimously raised their voices deploring the so-called "failure of multiculturalism."[5] It does not come as a surprise that Breivik quotes them approvingly,[6] at least on that score.

What we see here, is definitely a case of widely shared responsibility: The use of power and influence to shape ideas for action. That is the realm of politics.

Obviously, the line from choirs singing the failure of multiculturalism to Breivik is tenuous and indirect. More tenuous and indirect, to be sure, than the one between Sarah Palin's campaign ad with a gun scope's crosshairs placed over Gabrielle Giffords' Arizona district (with the message "Don't retreat, reload"), and Giffords' assassination attempt during a political meeting near Tucson on 8 January 2011 (an attempt that cost the lives of six others). But a line there is. Hence, a form of complicity. To understand this better, we must squarely enter the topic of politics.

Politics – and where it's gone

Angela Merkel may have been the only prominent European leader to take an almost heroically liberal view on immigration in recent years. Yet, even she was not immune to a tendency to accommodate socially divisive thinking that threatens to undermine democratic processes. There are no societies without tensions. But bearers of public authority, on all sides, must do whatever they can to defuse them. There is only one guiding principle that guarantees success in such efforts: openness to diversity. You are not the only one who would object, even if only with questions: How does that principle relate to democracy? And how could even Merkel have violated it if she welcomed hundreds of thousands of refugees in 2015 and 2016?

You are free to accuse me of dogmatism, but as long as there is no better instrument available, I am unwilling to regard any state or any political movement as democratic unless it demonstrably adheres to the rules laid down in the Universal Declaration of Human Rights, however strong its scent of historically Eurocentric morality may be. The rights to which the declaration pertains, are meant to count equally and inalienably for "all members of the human family." Just about all its articles begin with "All," "Everyone," or "No one." This means that the level at which compliance can be evaluated is the individual – the unique confluence of multiple dimensions of diversity: Age, gender, sexual orientation, physical appearance, health, language, social background, descent, nationality, country of origin, ethnicity, education, profession, status, religion, lifestyle. The quality of a democracy depends less on voting rights – essential as they may be – than on the extent to which it is open to diversity along all these dimensions. This principle is violated as soon as any society's dominant majority – however defined – imposes its own self-declared culture- or identity-related set of norms and values beyond those that reflect basic human rights or their operationalization by means of local law.

Is this advocacy for cultural relativism? Really not. Could it be used to defend sati, the practice of widow burning, or female circumcision? Not at all, as everyone should enjoy the right to life and everyone's physical integrity should be protected. Could it be used to defend violations of gender equality? Could it be used to impose religion-based legislation on anyone not sharing the same beliefs? Absolutely not, since every individual has the right to equal treatment, and no one can be subjected to the dictates of someone else's worldview. What the principle does imply, however, is the type of relativism that underlies the basic respect that enables you to openly discuss interpretations, practical arrangements, and consequences as soon as the issue of norms and values arises within and beyond democratically established legislation.

This principle is seriously endangered by the popular, politically fostered and fueled, simplistic attack on multiculturalism. Surely, in the later years of the 20th century you may have met people who naively celebrated diversity for its own sake. No doubt there were some, and they may have made sure that they were visible. The attack on multiculturalism, however, lives by the false presumption that its core was the comfortable flower-power celebration of everything-goes. Its essence, rather, was no more than the mere acceptance of the reality of diversity which, as every other aspect of human life, causes a set of issues that we must cope with as positively and as creatively as possible. And yes, you may have met people who were mistakenly thinking about these issues at the level of largely juxtaposed and relatively homogeneous groups, members of which only mingled occasionally during cultural fests organized specifically for that purpose. But they were clearly a minority. Rather, misguided group-based thinking is the source of the critique of multiculturalism, missing the target by many miles. In the words of Willem Schinkel (2018), the putatively "failed multiculturalism" is no more than a fiction, far removed from what was ever implemented or even proposed in places such as Western Europe.

It is a bit tragic that some of the truly realistic multiculturalists of the late 20th century let themselves be diverted to the new notion of "superdiversity."[7] This must have been a somewhat desperate (though intrinsically laudable) attempt to underscore the reality of diversity. An awareness of this reality and its inevitability was progressively getting erased by waves of newly invigorated nationalism. The notion must also have been motivated by the need to overcome the non-recognition of the fundamentally individual locus of the social dynamics involved in societal diversity. It is obviously the case that the shape of current diversity and the corresponding patterns of behavior are strongly affected by the twin features of increased mobility and versatile communication technologies. But the phenomenon of diversity as we now know it is not new in any fundamental sense.

People move more rapidly today, may stay in one place for shorter periods of time, and find it easier to live transnationally. Members of the same extended family may be scattered across countries, some as permanent residents, some on a tourist or student visa (perhaps outstaying their official welcome), others as refugees or asylum seekers. Within each of those categories, bonds may be forged with partners in fortune or misfortune with completely different backgrounds. But the ultimate measure of diversity remains the social and cultural positioning of the individual displaying multiple identities, which are not necessarily stable during a lifetime, and which one does not necessarily control oneself. Therefore, *societies are superdiverse by definition and have always been* – just as, for that matter, culture is always "multi" (not only incorporating multiple influences but also manifesting itself in myriad forms, so that "multiculturalism" was already an equally unfortunate tautological coinage). By launching the new term, the inevitability and perennial nature of this reality risks remaining underappreciated. At the same time, a current state of affairs gets dramatized out of proportion by the suggestion of exceptional degrees of fragmentation – providing ample fodder for all those who prefer to continue promoting the delusional comfort of life opposing "us" to "them."

Since the turn of the millennium, self-declared progressive intellectuals (in a strangely echoic relation to right-wing populist discourse) have been busily overtrumping each other with depictions of the "leftist" multiculturalists of the 1990s as naïve, irresponsible, and ultimately at the root of unresolved societal tensions (cf. Vertovec & Wessendorf 2010). As the story goes, multiculturalism was a monolithic dogmatic doctrine, supported far too long by the bureaucracies of Western states fearful of being labeled xenophobic. It promoted essentialist separation, segregation, even "balkanization," of different ethnic groups and undermined any attempt to promote social cohesion based on common values – culturally relativistic to the point of being supportive of reprehensible practices such as forced marriages and honor killings. Its proponents made debate impossible, denied problems, and thus spread a bed for terrorism – all in the name of their untouchable political correctness. But now a "new realism" (Prins's 2002 term) is finally emerging to overcome all that. Unpleasant truths can be spoken: "ethnic minorities simply fail to integrate; look at their overrepresentation in crime statistics, unemployment levels, school drop-out rates; the time has come to make them fulfill their duties in exchange for all the rights they enjoy." Do you recognize the pattern?

This is the line of reasoning, nowhere near uncommon, that is adduced to legitimate politicians' eager declaration of the failure of multiculturalism. True failure, however, resides in the proven inability of the powers that be to turn the tide of new (or old?) forms of nationalism. These have long since lost the ability to play an emancipatory role, a role that cannot be denied for specific "nationalist" movements at specific moments in history. They have become obsessively assimilationist – under the fashionable pretext of inclusiveness – if not downright exclusionist. Ever since the early 1990s, in many European countries, the extreme right has been setting the agenda. With ever-increasing speed, exclusionist premises and the stigmatization of difference have become the common fare of public rhetoric. Naturally, tensions have been growing. *People with power and influence, politicians and intellectuals alike, can no longer escape a charge of complicity.* Some have contributed consciously and willingly to this development. Others have not done enough to fight it. In between, there are the shadow boxers imagining themselves embroiled in a heroic struggle defending diversity while staying clear of any danger (by speaking "the truth" about the wrong type of diversity and effectively supporting an assimilationist agenda).

You may think that I am exaggerating. But just look at the country I am living in. At the time of writing this paragraph, the Belgian Parliament had just passed a new "foreigner law" which – in violation of my probably naïve understanding of the Constitution – enabled the expatriation of non-Belgians suspected of ties with terrorism or, more vaguely, of being a serious risk for the public order, even without proven guilt, and even if they were born in Belgium.[8] Also, a member of parliament seriously proposed – fortunately bumping into enough opposition – not to grant Belgian citizenship to children born in Belgium if one of the parents was not Belgian; a citizenship test would have to be passed at the age of eighteen. And basic rights to a professional defense were under pressure, as lawyers could now be fined if a foreigner whom they were defending got convicted of fraudulent use of social services.

Moving beyond the legal sphere, the Belgian Secretary of State for Asylum and Migration, Theo Francken, seemed unimpeachable despite a Facebook post in which he compared the "Jewish, Chinese and Indian diaspora" with "Moroccan, Congolese and Algerian migrants," saying that he could imagine some economic added value for the first group, but much less for the second. He also criticized Doctors without Borders for picking up boat refugees in the Mediterranean, accusing them of supporting illegal immigration. Similarly, the Flemish Minister for Integration and Equal Opportunities, Liesbeth Homans, is well-known for her claim that "racism is relative," and that it is used too often as an excuse for personal failure. Her federal counterpart, Belgian Secretary of State for Equal Opportunities Zuhal Demir, daughter of a first-generation immigrant family, presented herself as proof of the fact that in Belgium there are opportunities for everyone, if you are willing to take them. Immediately after assuming office she attacked UNIA, the federal agency for the fight against discrimination and racism, for being too concerned about the fate of "allochthons."[9] A couple of weeks later she found it appropriate to call the Christian-democratic CD&V a "Muslim party," failing to be sufficiently critical of Islam in order to be able to use Muslims as "ballot-box cattle" (*kiesvee*). Unfortunately, these are not just anecdotal examples, historically situated in 2017 and early 2018, and thus at first sight with passing relevance. They are representative of a general atmosphere of culpability surrounding "others," which stretches far beyond Belgium. Witness the growth of restrictions on personal freedom, often ethnically targeted in practice, which Shami Chakrabarti (2014) describes for the post–9/11 UK. Or Angela Davis' (2012) testimony to unresolved issues of freedom in the United States.

I will come back to these issues a little later, going beyond anecdotes. The burning question is: Where does this willingness come from to remain complicit, to share responsibility directly or indirectly, in the creation or maintenance of eruptive tensions? Why do people in positions of power and authority contribute ammunition – whether "on purpose" or not – rather than to defuse? My diagnosis does not count for truly autocratic regimes, which require an analysis of their own. What is looming large in the free societies of the "Global North," is *the dark side of representative democracy: Politicians practicing meta-politics*, most notably by orienting themselves exclusively to the arid landscape of the popular vote at election time.

I assume that political concerns, truly oriented to the common good, should try to steer away from preoccupations with vested interests, seek to diagnose structures and processes affecting members of society in adverse ways, and be in search of sustainable remedies. Politics at a meta-level, by way of contrast, has two defining features.[10] First of all, rather than to formulate disinterested diagnoses and remedies, politicians – with the help of spin doctors – construct their message around easy-to-remember slogan-like analyses of complex social realities which they imagine (often with good reason) to be powerful enough to convince a significant portion of the electorate (preferably a majority). For such meta-political perception management, staying "on message" or projecting a coherent image is more important than accurately presenting facts, carefully defining issues, and building consistent arguments.[11] Second, some politicians then go the extra mile to frame themselves as the only true representatives of "the people," often conveniently opposed to an estranged, snooty and self-centered cultural, intellectual, economic, political "elite" (a category to which, by any objective standards, they usually belong themselves). This profile is commonly referred to as populism.[12]

Populism goes hand in hand with polarization, as (an appearance of) public support is easier to achieve with simple messages than with sophisticated analyses. The prototypical example in recent history may be Donald Trump's demonstration of how even blatant lies, repeated often enough, may incite violent action, as when the MAGA mob raided the US Capitol on 6 January 2021. Repeat performances or echoes of this outrageous outcome of so-called democratic processes are not impossible. More harmful, in the long run, may be politicians' assumptions about public opinion which end up dictating their actions against their own better judgment. It is not uncommon to see U-turns in policy, implicitly or explicitly attributed to a "realistic assessment" of the popular mood. More often than not, easily manipulable emotions are exploited in the pursuit of ideologically inspired objectives. It does not seem to matter that contradictory positions are taken, depending on the policy area concerned. A strategic and selective *culture of doubt or denial*, discursively minimizing risks, seems to dictate the positioning of too many powerful politicians in critical areas affecting everyone, such as global warming or the spread of a pandemic. In future analyses, the (mis)management of the COVID-19 crisis from early 2020 all the way into 2021 will serve as a textbook example of politicians erratically moving in whatever direction they thought could foster their own public standing. Minimizing the risks or offering false prospects was too often the bottom line. This is hardly compatible with the *culture of fear*, discursively maximizing risks, that is consciously and successfully mobilized in the approach to the threat of migration or terrorism.[13] But, for the time being, it works. The reason why this works is simply that human thought or decision-making is less rational than Enlightenment philosophers would like it to be. People tune in to what directly appeals to them – and this reflex cannot even be said to be completely irrational. For politicians it suffices to find the proper vibrations.

Populists like Donald Trump, Marine Le Pen, Viktor Orbán, Geert Wilders, or Jair Bolsonaro are not the only ones practicing politics at a meta-level. Populist ideas and tactics are adopted and adapted wholesale. Twenty-first-century nationalists play hardball. They are usually on the offensive, dictating the terms of the debate. When under attack, they do not shy away from historical nonsense such as calling Nazism a leftist ideology. But they do not have a monopoly on facile political analyses and solutions that are expected to be palatable.

Remember Dutch socialist Diederik Samsom's proposal in early 2016, obviously seeking the wavelength of widespread anti-immigration sentiments, to immediately ferry back refugees arriving on the Greek islands from Turkey – a proposal applauded by many others, including Flemish socialist party leader John Crombez and the Danish social democrats. This is the softball response. More or less the same game, but less powerpacked. There may, in fact, never have been a better softball player than Dutch Prime Minister Mark Rutte when he celebrated the victory of his VVD (*Volkspartij voor Vrijheid en Democratie*, "People's Party for Freedom and Democracy) over Wilders' PVV (*Partij voor de Vrijheid*, "Freedom Party") in the March 2017 elections by proclaiming that The Netherlands – after Brexit and after the American elections – had halted "the wrong kind of populism."

Admission? Denial? Complicity all the same. And you and me, the public, we generally go along without the kind of resistance that would be needed to threaten the *status quo*. The current state of the world, however, should have taught us that the shallow democracy sprouting from meta-politics does not result in peace and stability. It simply narrows political options to the range of imaginaries characteristic of easy-to-produce and easy-to-maintain popular ideologies related to triumphant nation-building and the troubled co-existence of different ethnic or cultural groups, both intra-nationally and internationally. In other words, meta-politics not only contrasts with "true" politics concerned with the common good by narrowing its scope to impression management. *Meta-politics restructures democratic public spheres and the discourses, practices, and institutions that inform them.*

You may think, by now, that I am a hopeless pessimist. Admittedly, I am not as optimistic as some who believe that the crisis of democracy can be solved by replacing elections with lotteries to assign responsibilities. I am also less optimistic than supporters of a strong switch towards deliberative or participatory democracy, relying on horizontal, collective agency rather than hierarchical political structures. There may be good arguments for a revolutionary move towards power by lottery, at certain levels of political action. There are certainly even better arguments to supplement the workings of representational democracy with a deliberative model. But deliberative decision-making is possible only on well-defined punctual issues, the implementation of which usually involves a lot of further decision-making of a managerial kind. Moreover, it requires time and extremely competent guidance, so that it cannot be used for day-to-day political management, and least of all for responding to an urgent crisis.[14] Practical measures to change the way in which parliaments are composed (say, lottery instead of ballots) or to take important political decisions (say, rounds of informed citizen deliberation rather than only a session in parliament), consequential and momentous as they may be, would seem less important than the badly needed changes in political thought and ethics, which are needed to make reform possible in the first place, to install a democratic architecture oriented to common problem solving and, ideally, consensus.

Staying "on message" may be important for political success. But contrary to what may appear from populist meta-political practice, the content of messages to "stay on" has not become less important for any truly political positioning. But *where has the politics gone?* In extreme cases, more efforts seem to go into government formation – always with electoral goals in mind – than into governing. Somehow, a non-populist counter-movement has so far lacked the ability to frame its own message in ways that can appeal to a sufficiently broad popular base, and – more importantly – that does not look like a follow-up on the agenda set in the leading populist discourse. *Content is gradually evaporating with the advance of politics at the meta-level.* This is, basically, what has been happening with the weak leftist reactions to rightist movements across Europe in the past 25–30 years. The exclusionary agenda (sometimes called, without intended irony, "inclusive nationalism") has been consistently set by the right. The essence, everyone's unquestionably equal right to "human" life, did not survive unmangled.

Nor does democratic politics itself escape unharmed. By way of example, the assumption that decisiveness may attract approval makes it possible for even a "decommissioned" acting government to decide to go to war, as happened with the Belgian participation in NATO's offensive in Libya in 2011. When it really matters, debate is too often virtually absent, and protest remains deafeningly silent. When meta-politics dominates, truly democratic decision-making becomes redundant. However, so many of us are directly or indirectly involved, even when keeping silent, that it is hard to avoid the conclusion that complicity reigns.

Despite the obvious power that we keep giving them, politicians, especially in smaller states, have recently been portrayed as powerless puppets on the strings of international conventions. Indeed, predominantly neoliberal principles and structures safeguarding the interests of multinational corporations constrain the space within which local authorities maneuver. But the conventions themselves are made by politicians and approved by local parliaments. They cannot shirk their responsibility. They can indeed reclaim power. Usually, however, they only do so for the wrong reasons. Remember "Make America Great Again," or, for that matter, the Brexiteers' "Take back control." With the meta-political focus on a manipulated popular mood instead of the substance of political decision-making, clarity can only be achieved through simplicity. Is that, perhaps, the reason why a significant part of the electorate increasingly loses interest, becomes undecisive, or drifts towards extremes?

Derailed reflexivity

The practice of meta-politics is firmly grounded in human nature. Homo sapiens would not be who s/he is without reflexivity. I am using the term simply to refer to our ability to imagine, correctly or not, what is happening in other people's minds. We adapt what we say and do to such imaginings. Our identity depends to a large extent on how (we think) others see us. We want to achieve goals that must be mediated by others' reactions to who (they think) we are and what we do. Without reflexive awareness we would not be able to use language as we know it. Our inability to express fully explicitly what we mean condemns us to tentative hypotheses about what we need to say to be understood. But it is the ability to make such hypotheses that enables us to speak and build societies. Without this ability, also, we would not be able to pass on culture and knowledge, nor would we be able to collaborate in complex joint ventures (cf. Tomasello 1999). In other words, reflexivity makes us what and who we are as social beings.

A serious problem emerges, however, when activities in the public sphere – as already suggested – begin to unfold primarily at a meta-level dictated less by the intrinsic value of goals to be achieved than by considerations of what is necessary to obtain or maintain a position of power enabling one to achieve goals in the first place, whatever their value. In a traditional liberal democracy, laws are not made, or measures are not taken, without the support of a majority. But since not every citizen is directly involved in decision-making processes, a majority may be simply "constructed." It may be indicative of a dominant line of thinking within a class of politicians, based on their assumption of probable popular support that can be translated into (the maintenance of) political power. The result may be a set of policies that are not necessarily guided by the conviction that they would really, objectively, effectively address societal issues head-on. Such policies may nevertheless be presented as ultra-democratic attempts to do exactly what the people want, to do precisely what is in the people's interest. Yet, they may be merely constructions based on what politicians think a significant segment of the population could possibly want or easily be persuaded of.

This is where reflexivity goes into overdrive or derails. Note that "reflexivity" is a valid analytical category to explain how the human mind-in-society works.[15] The term refers to a social reality, an observable process. "Derailed reflexivity," by contrast, is a moral category – though not less useful for identifying what happens in society. The term does not refer to a different kind of process, a different phenomenon. It designates a way of over-using (or, as we shall also see later, of willfully under-using) the powers of reflexivity, which may have detrimental effects. You may think of it as overshooting (or deliberately missing) a target, with all the resulting risks.

A slightly amusing example came up in the aftermath of the terrorist attacks in Brussels in March 2016. The Belgian government decided to deploy heavily armed soldiers to patrol sensitive areas in a few cities. In the words of Antwerp mayor Bart De Wever, they would be the only ones with "the necessary operational firepower." But, for one thing, this is mostly security theater (cf. Schneier 2003), as everyone knows that a couple of paratroopers are not going to stop a suicide bomber. What is more, their presence marks potentially interesting targets for the hypothetical would-be terrorist at a loss to find one. So, this measure mainly serves the culture of fear as a display of strong resolve, on the assumption that this is what the public wants. Some welcome it, while for many others it heightens the sense of insecurity. Reflexivity already derails at that point. But there is more. At a certain moment, a couple of soldiers were spotted wearing a scarf looking like a Palestinian keffiyeh, which they had apparently brought with them as a souvenir from an earlier mission abroad. Immediately, an army spokesperson profusely apologized in an uncalled-for public statement. No-one had raised objections (yet). But the idea that someone might think of objecting based on a potential impression of provocation was clearly enough to jumpstart an anticipatory response-controlling media effort.

Politics is only one of the domains where reflexivity goes into overdrive; others will pass the review later, namely educational institutions and the media. Nor is this development unique to the current period in history. Yet, the early 1990s initiates an age of systematically derailing reflexivity that will run through the rest of this book as a *leitmotiv*, without claiming that this would represent anything entirely new.

The public sphere, which I understand as any space of publicly accessible meaning and therefore as an arena for struggles over meaning, may always have been asymmetrical. Whereas true dialogue requires intersubjective involvement and reciprocity, and is therefore mostly confined to small-scale private interaction, the public sphere provides spectacle from a distance and has many more spectators than actors. That is why Ari Adut (2018) calls it a realm of "appearances."

Political spectacle has evolved with the affordances of technology. Richard Bauman (2013) described how William Jennings Bryan adapted political rhetoric twice during the US presidential election campaigns of 1896 and 1908. In 1896 he introduced the whistle-stop tours, using the expanded reach of the railroads to address multiple audiences with brief speeches adjustable to specific contexts, emphasizing contact over argument. In 1908 he used the new communicative technology of the phonograph, recording his speeches, necessarily expository in style and minimizing contextual specificity to be maximally recontextualizable. This was a far cry from currently available tools. But asymmetry remains, even with the use of modern means of communication which, in principle, enable everyone to "participate." The most tangible effect of the technological innovations exemplified by Facebook and Twitter is the uncontrollable diversification of audiences, a thoroughly fragmented public sphere that no doubt requires extra reflexive attention for purposes of manipulation, publicity, or simply monitoring. Uncontrollable, I just said? In principle, yes. In practice, everyone's "participation" makes it possible to harvest – even if illegally – individual beliefs and inclinations, thus enabling micro-targeted propaganda, so that different messages reach different people, and no ordinary citizen can keep track of the information (true or false) fed to communities they do not themselves belong to. Remember Cambridge Analytica (see Briant, 2021).

Derailed reflexivity may to a certain extent follow from the loss of control – which was always more illusory than real – over the composition of the audience to be addressed in public discourse. But it definitely is also a by-product of so-called neoliberalism (cf. Monbiot 2016, Springer 2016, Springer et al. 2016). Perhaps it is better to simply talk about true or "liberated" liberalism taking the form of "globalized capitalism" (a point well-argued by Badiou 2016). It is globalized in the sense of spread across the globe or liberated from the restrictions imposed by states (i.e., "deregulated"). It is also globalized in the sense of ever-expanding control over society-organizing capabilities of the human mind prevailing in domains beyond the economic.

Be that as it may, when competition comes to define social relations, as it does in this (neo)liberal or globalized capitalist world, there are winners and losers. Identifying them requires monitoring and assessment. These activities at a meta-level would be extremely useful if the purpose would be to lay bare and to remedy inequalities in the playing field. The rules of the game, however, are hegemonic and remain unquestioned. Equality of opportunity functions as a foundational myth, a far cry from the capability-based egalitarianism envisioned by Sen (1992). Identification of the winners is followed by praise. Losers, while outnumbering the winners, are chided – they did not make optimal use of the chances they got. By some, the norms of the market ideology may have been sufficiently appropriated to result in easy self-praise and (probably more hesitant) self-blaming. To be successful politically, a populist must be able to exploit pride, as well as frustration and anger, by means of simple messages that project continued success or illusionary deliverance from a state of hopelessness. You will not easily forget, once more, "Make America Great Again." This is meta-politics of the highest rank. Explanations for why millions voted for Trump are easy to evoke. We may even truly understand. But it is important to realize that *apologetic empathy is a close cousin to genuine complicity.*

You may wonder whether there is an alternative. There is. Truly democratic political concern, no matter whether it is organized in a traditional state-based representational form or in combination with horizontally structured collective deliberation efforts, would address inequality. You must know by now that, roughly speaking, 1% of the world population possesses nearly half of the world's wealth, the top 10% owns 86%, the next 40% divides the remaining 14%, and the bottom half of the people of the world have virtually nothing at all. Globalized capitalism, benefiting from the weakening of states, cannot be expected to change this for the better. Political decisions must be taken. But to do so, for instance in a European context, the European Union should shed its current nature as supranational vehicle of liberated liberalism and turn itself into a structure, perhaps a democratic "state," that is strong enough to withstand the unchecked development of semi-autonomous capitalist forces. Such a transformation would be revolutionary. It would require the courage to admit that whatever social security can be provided for people will be increasingly at their own expense – unless unchained capital can be brought under control. But even if the transformation would succeed, there is a serious risk that such a structure or "state" would fail to look beyond its borders.

The reason for such failure is the existence of a type of inequality that is not measurable in economic terms and that results from habits of thought according to which "we" are the center of civilization. One symptom is, for instance, that clear thinking about guilt and responsibility for crimes, even about complicity, seems to stop when so-called "Islamic terror" creates generalized suspicion towards Islam. You know there is no objective reason for this: 1.6 billion people are Muslims, and a vast majority condemns terrorism. By the same token, as we have seen, terror may be rooted in just about any form of extremism or despair. And any religion may lend itself as an excuse, including Christianity. Remember the complex mix of secular and religious factors upholding Franco's brutal fascism way beyond the carnage of World War II, or, until more recently, energizing the vortex of violence in the Northern Irish "Troubles." Or bear in mind the resurgence of religiously inspired intolerance for non-heteronormative sexuality, from Russian cities where it is not safe for gays and lesbians to walk, over mass-demonstrations against same-sex marriage in France, or the distribution of "LGBT-free zone" stickers in Poland, to the persistent attacks on LGBTQIA+ rights by Christian fundamentalists in the US – the potential for violence, if not violence itself, is never far away.

After waves of secularization in the earlier 20th century (Kemal Atatürk's Turkey, Gamal Abdel Nasser's Egypt, Jawaharlal Nehru's India, Mohammad Reza Pahlavi's Iran, even – though more hesitantly – David Ben Gurion's Israel), religion has been rapidly regaining territory in the public sphere as a polarizing and potentially "de-secularizing" force. Not only in the Muslim world. Witness Narendra Modi's Hindu nationalism in India, the strengthening religious Jewish identity of Israel, the growing political influence of orthodox spirituality in post-Soviet Russia and of Catholicism in Poland, the revival of militant Buddhism in Myanmar.

Yet, it is generalized suspicion of Islam, extended into more profound non-acceptance of diversity, that is exploited by a not-so-democratic meta-political leadership and easily swallowed by significant portions of Western populations. Just observe, with me, some of the political measures controlling ways of living, freedom of movement, language use, and even the sense of identity, which are not halted by protest. And keep asking whether, perhaps, we share responsibility for processes of meta-political derailment.

Enlightened condescension

The debate about what Muslim women should or should not wear seems not to be going away. In stark contrast to selectively immigration-friendly countries such as Canada, where a Minister of Defense can go about performing his public duties wearing a turban,[16] there are numerous places in Europe forbidding women to cover their hair in public institutions, at municipal service counters, in schools or hospitals. Headscarves or hijabs are associated with Islam. Wearing them, so the reasoning goes, violates principles of laicism or secularism in public life. I hope you are inclined to ask, as I would, whether the absence of religious symbols really is more neutral than the visible presence of a divergent range of them. In my worldview, neutrality neither obliges nor forbids. It leaves you free. Laicism began as a cry for pluralism, not uniformity, the secular state not as neutral but as visibly plural. Yet, in a perverse extension of the laicism argument beyond the public domain, private companies – fortunately with significant exceptions – have followed the example of municipal and national authorities. They also invoke neutrality to legitimate their vestmental injunctions while, as you know, the real reason is purely commercial: The fear of losing customers who take offence at the recognizability of a Muslim woman.

Sometimes, institutions must take difficult decisions. Wearing a jilbab or hijab, or a more radically disguising niqab or burqa, as a token of gender inequality and male coercion, is a stereotypical image. Stereotype or not, it is sometimes real. In demonstrable cases of generalized coercion, and after serious but ineffective attempts to turn the tide of (usually male) despotism, one can imagine the prohibition of headscarves as a protective measure in a specific institutional context. But because of the essential paradox, and because of the rigid conditions for justification, any truly democratic position would assume that prohibition must be highly exceptional. The rule is individual freedom. No one can be wantonly denied the right to personal authority over her own free will. And still, this happens in the democracies of the 21st century.

Before developing this line of reasoning further, here is a little anecdote to illustrate how truly anti-Islamic the anti-headscarf sentiments really are. Decades after the classical hospital caps for nurses had gone out of use, Muslim women employed in Flemish hospitals were first denied the right to cover their heads while at work. Arguments went from "not practical" to "not hygienic." Until one hospital found a trick to meet the Muslim women's demands without getting weighed down by Islamic symbolism. They reintroduced the classical hospital cap. A traditional headscarf was out of the question. The cap, with the logo of the hospital, was not a problem. Everybody was happy: Muslim women could keep their heads covered; other employees, patients, and visitors did not associate this new uniform item with Islam but with a traditional hospital style. Minor detail: The style of the hospital cap was reminiscent, for those old enough, of a Catholic nun's attire.

The "Western" model of separation between state and church was not originally anti-religious (cf. Demiati 2009). It was anti-Vatican or anti-clerical, rising from the legitimate struggle of lay people to constrain the political power of the (Catholic) church. Now the principle of laicism is invoked in a fight against Islam, a putative enemy without local worldly power. The ambition which some undoubtedly cherish to acquire such power is more effectively countered by education and the strengthening of non-discriminatory democratic mechanisms. Unequal treatment, even at the level of the state, now goes unnoticed. Islamic leaders are systematically scrutinized by national security services. In Belgium, recent efforts to start the local training of imams were not presented as meeting the rights of an officially recognized religious community, but rather as a dam against "foreign" political-religious influences and radicalization.

But no one objects when Western heads of state pay quasi-obligatory visits to the Pope – not as the ruler of the Vatican, a miniature state of negligible geopolitical importance, but foremost as influential religious leader. Western heads of state also enjoy meeting the Dalai Lama. In contrast to the Pope, he has until recently been more openly approached as the banned political leader of Tibet than as spiritual leader of Tibetan Buddhism. While he was combining the two functions, no one asked him – mindful of the principle of laicism – whether these were in fact compatible.

Generalized suspicion against Islam has led to at least one piece of vestmental legislation in some European countries. The complete or partial prohibition of burqa or niqab in public spaces is carefully dissociated from Islam by formulating laws in terms of "face-covering garments" in general.

For official purposes there are indeed situations when it is necessary to be able to identify a person. But, so the reasoning goes, when a person is not recognizable in the street, in public buildings, on bus, tram, or train, at least a sense of insecurity arises. Yet, the same reasoning does not seem to hold when facial disguises are not reminiscent of Islam. Therefore, a few exceptions are stipulated at once: Motorcycle helmets, carnival masks, professional safety gear, or customary clothing habits (no doubt including the balaclavas designed to anonymize the members of police intervention teams, which do not necessarily generate a sense of safety).

So, the law does not look as non-anti-Islamic as it is passed off by its proponents. Predictably, the law will become void as soon as the COVID-19 pandemic or its successors lead to generalized acceptability of face masks in public, as has been the case for a long time in countries such as Japan, where they simply belong to good manners for anyone with even a common cold. You will agree that in specific types of contexts communication preferably involves a literal face-to-face encounter. When seeking legal or medical advice, you may prefer not to talk to someone with a carnival mask, a motorcycle helmet, or – indeed – a burqa, though again COVID-19 may score its face-covering effects. The argument that a person must be recognizable certainly cannot be invoked to justify the ban which some French coastal municipalities have imposed on the wearing of so-called burkinis on the beach (which rarely cover the wearer's face). How can someone's body-covering clothing be experienced as threatening, except by association with Islam and generalized suspicion?

Progressive proponents of a ban on headscarves in institutional or public contexts are under serious pressure to show that it does not violate freedom of religion. Therefore, rationalizations continue. Because not all Islamic women cover their hair and/or face, so the argument goes, this concerns a cultural or regional tradition and not a religious norm. Yet some legal directives, in a spirit of generosity, stipulate explicitly that spaces and buildings serving religious purposes must be exempt from a ban. What can justify such exemption other than the open admission that at least for some people a religious norm is involved? Here an interesting tension emerges. By contrasting religious norms with cultural and regional traditions, diversity gets denied as soon as a religion receives a homogenizing label. In general, there is a theoretical awareness of the many divergent manifestations of Islam. But this awareness is nicely tucked aside when it threatens to undermine the legitimation for the imposition of desirable behavior.

The crowning touch which pulls along a significant number of progressive people in their support for bans on headscarves in institutional contexts (or, *a fortiori*, burqas in public spaces), is the argument that these garments symbolize the inequality of men and women, so that an injunction serves to protect women. Wearers are not asked whether they cover their hair or their faces voluntarily. Their claims to that effect, according to the self-proclaimed heirs of the Enlightenment, betray a lack of awareness that in fact they only do so under coercion from men. You will agree that social pressure may be an important element, and that coercion must be countered. But the new laws and regulations, without any form of dialogue, deny the free will of those concerned and plunge them into the isolation against which protection is said to be intended. Moreover, these laws and regulations are merely symbolic: Burqas are extremely exceptional in a Western environment, no one has seriously tried to impose them in communicative contexts absolutely requiring facial recognition, and an injunction would no longer work if the practice of wearing them would pass the threshold of its current marginality.

Gender equality serves as the main argument in all areas in which the need for a separation between church and state cannot be invoked. Global injunctions in view of protection bear witness, ironically, to a lack of faith in the deliberative capacities or personal accountability of women. The avowed mission is to bring them into "our" modernity, where everyone is supposed to make personal and rational choices, ignoring that this is a mythical, unattained ideal goal detached from social reality in just about every dimension of our own behavior. The message is gift-wrapped enlightened condescension rather than a genuine plea for equality, i.e., the perversion of a valuable fundamental principle.

How could freedom, equality, religious and political pluralism – the true tenets of the separation between church and state – be threatened by an individual service provider's wearing tokens of personal conviction while performing official duties? You may not want to see the walls of public service counters, courtrooms, or public schools, adorned with crucifixes or any other religious or partisan symbols. But the neutrality of an institution is heightened by visible plurality. It is certainly not undermined by the recognizable positioning of its employees. Nor is this the claim of proponents of a ban. The more subtle argument is that all perception or suspicion of partiality or prejudice should be avoided. But even this betrays boundless lack of trust. First, whoever assumes that a man with kippah, a woman with a headscarf, a service provider with a lapel pin cross, a policeman with a turban, would be inclined not to treat everyone equally, does not believe in the tolerance and pluralist openness of Jews, Muslims, Christians, or Sikhs. Second, whoever ascribes such assumptions to those requiring services unmistakably doubts the ability of the average citizen to see "Others" as ordinary human beings and fellow citizens conscientiously performing specific public roles. Condescension on all fronts. With a heavy burden of responsibility, not just indirect complicity, on the part of a significant part of the self-described progressive intelligentsia.

Headscarf or not? That may be an important question for the woman who looks in the mirror in the morning. But her answer should be inconsequential when she steps outside. In a world that respects personal freedom, neither approval nor condemnation should be called for. Unfortunately, our world is different. What should be trivial personal decisions turn into heated political debates. It is high time to get adapted to visible diversity in the public sphere, including far-ranging hybridity: "Westernized" Muslim women with headscarves, married Muslim gay men, "Western" men converted to Islam who refuse (like most orthodox Jewish men) to shake a woman's hand and to give preference to other signs of respect. These are all people subject to criticism from different corners of society. A society which cannot muster sufficient courage to enforce respect for such identities and personal choices, denying them visibility and equality in public life, cannot call itself democratic. It does not matter, then, whether the obstacles are imposed by an oppressive version of Islam, by a cultural or nationalistic reflex, or by enlightened condescension. Multiple layers of complicity are involved.

Walls and borders

People have roots, but only in a metaphorical sense. They are constantly in motion, even if only locally. And whenever there is an urgent need or a strong desire, they move outside of whatever is construed as their "home" territory. This need not cause friction with other people, but it may. Attempts at curbing migration, therefore, are as old as migration itself. In roughly 2,000 B.C., King Shulgi of Ur built a 250 km wall in Mesopotamia to keep out the nomad Amorites.[17] So there is nothing original about the Israeli West Bank barrier or Donald Trump's (largely imaginary) wall on the Mexico-US border. Among their illustrious precursors we find the Great Wall of Gorgan, Hadrian's Wall, the Great Wall of China. They all share a history of limited success. Not only do they all eventually outlive their purpose – a fate that also contemporary examples will not manage to escape. They also have their inherent weaknesses. The Amorites could simply walk around Shulgi's wall at both ends. Tunnels can be dug. Fences can be cut. Border guards can be bribed. Ironically, the most successful borders so far seem to have been those designed to keep people in rather than to keep people out: those of North Korea and former East Germany. The latter has already disappeared, the former will, one day.

A popular argument holds that an open society cannot function without its being protected by borders (cf. Scheffer 2016). You are right, in a negative sense this is true. As long as citizens (or denizens, for that matter) enjoy their rights under the protection of justice systems administered by states, even basic human rights can only be effectively protected by states.

International legal frameworks only come into existence thanks to willingness at the level of "national" entities. Whatever welfare and security people are entitled to must be organized; organization requires structures; if states are not the structures most suitable for such tasks, they must be replaced by others. Too often, however, this is used by the political right – with complicity from the left – to close borders or to only keep them barely ajar, sometimes in violation of the human rights the borders are supposed to protect.

For a recent example, look at what happened at the Greek-Turkish border in March 2020. Turkish President Recep Erdoğan told Syrian refugees they could cross into the European Union, using them in a cynical attempt to exert pressure in a political dispute. Greece kept the border closed under the helicopter-borne approving gaze of the Presidents of the European Council (Charles Michel) and the European Commission (Ursula von der Leyen). Refugees were treated on water cannons, tear gas, and rubber bullets, or bussed – in anonymized vehicles – to detention camps from which they were sent back, sometimes half-naked. Boats with refugees were literally pushed back into Turkish waters. And the right to apply for asylum was suspended. A clear violation of human rights, of the type we are so keen to accuse others of.

The rhetoric that rich countries "cannot simply alleviate all the misery of the world or welcome every poverty-stricken or persecuted Asian or African" is a highly politicized platitude only used to nourish the culture of fear. Even with today's means of mobility only 3% of the world's population lives outside the borders of the country they are citizens of. Of those, the vast majority lives in a neighboring country. Those who arrive in the rich "Global North" are not predominantly the poor masses, but often the small segment that can afford to pay for long-distance travel and that is usually already well-connected in an international diaspora. Among "illegal" foreigners, two-thirds arrived legally and simply overstay their visas. Furthermore, migration is a thoroughly circular phenomenon. People do not only come in. People also leave. Expatriates are also migrants, and their circulation can be traced: France sent doctors and nurses to Switzerland and Canada, welcoming doctors from the Maghreb and, for a while, nurses from Spain which, in turn, recruited nurses from Latin America.

The fear-mongering surrounding migration is an excellent example of quite successful politics at a meta-level. François Héran (2018) distinguishes three stages in French migration politics – and his distinctions can be extrapolated to many European countries. After a period of economically motivated policies, welcoming migrants as guest workers, immigration was halted around 1974 with the oil crisis which produced high levels of unemployment. Then a phase of judicially based migration policies set in: Immigrants successfully invoked their right to reunify their families.

Though both economic and legal motives are still in operation, today's migration policies mainly display the maneuvering of a politics of opinion (*la politique d'opinion*). The self-declared "true" representatives of the people use the largely unjustified, politically kindled, fear of migration in pursuit of electoral success. They profile themselves, therefore, as tough executors of the public will. Here reflexivity derails. Political stances derive justification from a public opinion that is itself the product of barely veiled demagoguery, and that may not even be as uniform and general as it is imagined (or wished) to be. There are plenty of people, no doubt, who would prefer politicians less obsessively concerned with the management of public opinion, but with the courage to act in accordance with the values we mostly pay lip service to.

The agenda is clearly set by the extreme right (recently euphemized as "radical" right), which does not hesitate now to go global, then to bend back onto its local self, depending on the inspiration of the moment. As to going global, an unofficial delegation of 23 members of the European Parliament (belonging to the likes of France's *Rassemblement national* and Germany's *Alternative für Deutschland*, sharing with Modi's Hindu nationalism mainly its islamophobia) visited Kashmir in October 2019. This visit took place just after the region had been divested of its autonomy and while the Indian government was barring access to foreign journalists and imposing an internet shutdown (cf. Leidig 2020).

As to bending back, feeling the hot breath of the extreme right *Vlaams Belang*, the Flemish nationalist *N-VA* (*Nieuw-Vlaamse Alliantie*) decided to pull out of the Belgian government when Prime Minister Charles Michel signed the *Global Compact for Migration* in Marrakesh in December 2018. They were certainly inspired by Donald Trump and Hungary's Viktor Orbán, who had already rejected the UN initiative earlier, followed by Austria's Sebastian Kurz, governing at that time in coalition with the extreme right FPÖ (*Freiheitliche Partei Österreichs*), and by Bulgaria, the Czech Republic, and Poland.

The intergovernmentally negotiated agreement, however, presented itself explicitly as "a non-legally binding, cooperative framework" (Article 7). But it also presupposed commitment to the UN's New York Declaration for Refugees and Migrants. Moreover, it was felt to speak too positively about migration by describing it as "a source of prosperity, innovation and sustainable development in our globalized world" (Article 8) where "[we are] all countries of origin, transit and destination" (Article 10). National sovereignty was included as a guiding principle (in Article 15). But critics regarded it as under threat, no doubt because the compact was also upholding principles such as "We must empower migrants to become full members of our societies, highlight their positive contributions, and promote inclusion and social cohesion" (Article 13). Entirely against the grain was Objective 17, "Eliminate all forms of discrimination and promote evidence-based public discourse to shape perceptions of migration" (further specified in Article 33). N-VA hardliners such as Theo Francken, then responsible for migration issues, hoped that trying to keep the Belgian government from signing, and by pulling out when it did, would translate into votes during the upcoming elections in May 2019. The effect, however, was more votes for the extreme right.

The not-so-extreme right has been trying to curb migration as best they can. Wherever you live, you will have seen examples. Public discourse is dominated by the feeling that there is always too much immigration, except when money is brought in supporting the local economy. There are never enough foreign investors. There are always too many foreigners. The factuality and necessity of migration are sometimes admitted. Every now and then even lyrical pieces appear about migration as a source of encounters and creativity. In museums and other cultural institutions, this message is allowed loud and clear. Charles Sandison's "The River," projecting a flow of 16,597 names of population groups, cultures, and geographical places related to the collections of the Parisian Musée du quai Branly (*là où dialoguent les cultures* – the place where cultures enter into dialogue) greatly impresses visitors since 2010.

Still, Europeans accept a law forbidding marriage migration from non-Western countries under the age of 24. Such a rule was introduced in Denmark in 2002. This was long before the Danish Social Democrats under Mette Frederiksen voted, in 2016, in favor of a law allowing police to seize refugees' assets (in particular, all "non-essential" items worth more than 10,000 Danish crowns without sentimental value to their owners). More recently, the Frederiksen government (in office since June 2019) introduced the so-called "ghetto-package" aimed at the redevelopment of "vulnerable" housing areas with too many inhabitants of non-Western origin. The goal is the protection of "Danishness."

Looking at my own country again, there is an abundance of dissuasive measures, such as planned structural shortages of housing for asylum seekers, rising registration fees for newcomers, or significant delays in access to social services. Once they are in, immigrants may encounter additional obstacles, such as extra taxes on night shops and shisha bars, defined as "image-lowering" businesses and predominantly run by minorities with a migration background. As long as residence permits are not in order, which may take a long time in the case of asylum procedures, they permanently run the risk of deportation. If a family manages to stay illegally – or by stretching legal procedures – after a negative decision, it may face expulsion even after many years of building up a productive and fully integrated life locally. The personal and social damage caused by such expulsions no doubt outweighs the marginal benefits of strictly imposing the law (cf. Carens 2010) – unless deterrence is the only goal.

As an ultimate dissuasive measure, politicians have been trying to outshine each other in the vigor with which they have declared that, under certain circumstances, immigrants should be robbed of their citizenship. Admittedly, the circumstances mentioned usually involve serious crime. But the measure can even be applied to second- and third-generation immigrants who have never been migrants at all. Leaving aside the problem of unequal treatment (different punishment for the same crimes), the basic message is "you do not really belong here."

Walls and borders do not have to be physical, not even juridical. They may be purely evaluative. The most charitable version is one in which the anticipation of problems prompts persons in authority to extend a helping hand to newcomers in ways that kindly but flatly identify them as outsiders. More common is the case of politicians referring to such benevolence as proof that (sons and daughters of) immigrants get all possible chances, that they should be grateful, and that they are themselves to blame for failure. This attitude is too often shared by successful people with a migration background.

One of the ingredients of evaluative border construction is the relativization of racism which holds not only that racism is too often used as an excuse for personal failure, but also that minority members are themselves often racist. This ignores completely the fact that racism, just like discrimination based on gender, scores negative effects only for those at the less powerful end of a relationship of dominance. At the other end, there is privilege.

Ignoring the walls erected by racism and xenophobia, even in their mildest forms, is a form of complicity that is far from innocent. It should worry you to see how racism and xenophobia are denied, minimized, or justified in discourse at the extreme and even not-so-extreme right of the political spectrum. Fortunately, justification is still relatively rare. When it raises its head, whether or not in the form of white supremacy movements, it thrives on references to the work of "race realists" who claim to have evidence for genetic differences responsible for divergencies in intelligence between population groups.[18] One of the currently influential "race realists" is the Canadian psychologist Jordan Peterson, a strong believer in the absolute measure of IQ tests and the "cognitive stratification of society" due to heritable, lasting, and irremediable differences in intelligence among racial or ethnic groups. In his view, hierarchy in society is determined by personal ability and accomplishments, not power.[19] It takes a genius to wipe out a history of racial discrimination (see, e.g., Zinn 2011) with the blunt instrument of a psychological test.

Sometimes ethnic profiling finds its legitimation in statistical correlations between ethnicity and crime. You know the statistics: Though black people represent only 2.8% of the UK population over 15 years of age, they form over 13% of the prison population; in the USA, almost a third of black men in their twenties are in prison, on parole or on probation; in Belgium people with non-European nationality, representing less than 5% of the population, are responsible for almost 20% of prosecuted crime cases.

These figures are all snapshots which vary from year to year, but the tendencies are clear. There is much less clarity about the causes, despite the abundance of theories. Socio-economic factors certainly cannot be discounted. Nor can a form of institutional bias which leads to more suspicion and more controls when police officers are confronted with members of specific minorities. Or very simple facts, such as US drug enforcement focusing strongly on crack (the cheaper, smokable form of cocaine), constituting only one third of drug transactions but heavily concentrated in the black American population, leaving white users of methamphetamine, xtc (MDMA), powder cocaine, and heroin relatively untouched (see Fellner 2009). In those cases, the walls you should be thinking of are those of a prison.

Meanwhile, racist discourse has become so normalized that, notwithstanding antiracist legislation, there are rarely consequential reactions. The only vocal and influential minority is the Jewish population, which is justly heard whenever there is a new case of antisemitism. But it is not impossible to hear a politician say during an election rally – with impunity – that today's problem is not that society becomes too grey, but rather that it is turning too brown.[20] Is it necessary to go to court every time? Maybe that is not the best strategy. But silence is complicity.

Of tongues ordinary and sublime

Language can be used as a border too. In 1983, US Senator S.I. Hayakawa, a professional linguist, launched *U.S. English*, an advocacy platform promoting legislation to make English the only official language of the United States. By 2016, already thirty-two states had some form of official English law. The purpose is to make English the only official language for public documents, records, legislation, official ceremonies, and public meetings. *U.S. English* emphasizes that this cannot be identified with an *English-only* movement, since "common-sense exceptions" would be permitted: For public health and safety services, judicial proceedings, foreign language instruction, the promotion of tourism. Yet, knowledge of English would be a prerequisite for full US citizenship. You will agree that the use of a common language can have a unifying role. It is not surprising, therefore, that similar movements can be found in many different places in the world. But this matter is not as simple as it seems at first sight.

Widespread belief in the reality of separable languages may be completely innocent. Promoting knowledge of a standardized version of a language may facilitate societal processes. But the innocence fades away, and the facilitating effects may be undermined, when an imagined order is imposed as the norm. Think, for instance, of territorial monolingualism as a guiding principle, imposed because of a nationalist ideology and in spite of far-ranging multilingualism as a social fact. The nationalist imagination can be stretched to the point where sizeable groups of so-called "other-linguals" are not recognized as a lasting social reality even after many decades.[21] This happens in my own small European region, Flanders, which unfortunately is not the only society displaying a steadfast problematization of bi- or multilingualism. By definition, according to popular thought, "other-linguals" have a language problem, and their language problem harms social cohesion. People fail to see the virtuosity with which immigrant children play around with multiple languages and language varieties, while often experiencing serious difficulties with the formal school language – a very specific register which is not only problematic for immigrant children (cf. Jaspers 2018). They ignore that monolingual territories, viewed from a global perspective, are exceptional and that also in Europe they have been created artificially and relatively recently (cf. Hobsbawm 1990).

Language is a universal human phenomenon, not more – nor less – than the result of biological development. Just like other biological processes, the development of language has led to a diversity of appearances. The degree of diversity, however, may very well exceed that of the physiological world because language, thanks to human cognitive capacities, can and must be mobilized for interaction in ever-changing contexts that cannot be reduced to a restricted set of parameters such as food and shelter, but that are characterized by complex social patterns, institutional restrictions, cultural and psychological variables.

Diversity conjures up images of chaos, the Tower of Babel, diversity as a handicap. Roughly estimated, and depending on how we count, there are more than 6,000 languages, very unevenly distributed across the earth, with an uneven distribution for the number of speakers, with countless forms of mixture, and with over seven billion idiolectal variants which literally promote language to everyone's individual property (in the sense of both quality and possession). But the chaos is treacherous. Language has universal features. There are no languages without vowels. Language does not require any iconic connection between a word and its meaning – the word "salt" does not taste like salt nor is it granular. Utterances have a linear structure – we cannot say two things at the same time. Language is always reflexive – we hear ourselves speak, interpret what we are saying ourselves, and form hypotheses about others' interpretations. Not a single utterance is fully explicit. And though there aren't two people who speak a fully identical language, we can communicate – for most purposes – thanks to shared principles and strategies to generate and negotiate meanings.

Thus, there is sufficient order in language. But there is also imagined order. Language is a natural phenomenon. But *a* language is always, without exceptions, an artificial construct, an abstraction. Our cognition requires categories to capture and handle the diversity of phenomena in the world. Therefore, we split the universal phenomenon of language up into different languages, plural. Language differences are of course experienced – you do not understand every human inhabitant of this planet. But in addition, *a* specific language is usually the product of political and ideological processes. Or, as the British say, a language is a dialect with an army and a navy. The British are experts on the matter. Thanks to their army and navy the empire was built which formed the basis for the present status of English as a world language. Yet, English itself shows the paradox of a universal language: The more a language spreads, the more internal diversity it will develop, the less universal it will be, and the harder it will become to speak of *a* language. Hence the various English*es*.

In an institutional context – social services, government administration, education, the judiciary – policies that refuse to adapt to the reality of multilingualism usually form a more serious problem than the multilingualism itself, even though indeed it requires (if seen from a monolingualism-as-norm point of view) extra effort, extra means, and extra attention. The incongruence between reality and policy has grave consequences: The problematization of a natural phenomenon (comparable to the denial of gravity), the stigmatization of those concerned, forms of exclusion based on deviations from a monolingual norm, and, as a result, social disadvantage.

Stigmatizing and discriminatory measures tend to pop up as a matter of course. They are presented as necessities and sometimes even as tokens of openness. For a good example I return once more to Flanders, the Dutch-speaking north of Belgium. You may wonder why, given the relative insignificance of this small European region. The reason is not only that I live there. But Belgium is rather unique with respect to language laws – laws that stipulate language obligations rather than language rights. Disregarding the bilingual status of Brussels and of a small German-speaking section of the south-eastern part of the country, there is a real language border, north of which the only official language is Dutch, and south of which the only official language is French. Changes in the actual composition of the population have no role to play, which keeps creating tensions in some of the municipalities surrounding Brussels. So, for example, there cannot be subsidized education in French north of the border, or in Dutch south of the border.

In Flanders, a decision was taken to link access to social housing to a command of Dutch: Basic proficiency in Dutch is formulated as an obligation for tenants. This requirement is based on three false premises. First, without coercion, "they" will not learn the local language. Second, under pressure they will. Third, as soon as they have an elementary command of the local language, communication problems fade away. The argument that denial of access to social housing based on a language criterion guarantees smooth communication and hence promotes social cohesion, misses a sense of reality. There is ample evidence that intercultural communicative friction is equally pervasive when the "same" language is spoken but without sufficient mutual awareness of elusive differences in communicative style generating harmful misinterpretations.[22] The argument also ignores the pernicious effects of stigmatization and discrimination.

You are not alone if you wonder how I can suggest that a measure intended to promote cohesion is in fact discriminatory. But how would you define cohesion and discrimination? Is cohesion not too often confused with homogeneity (as was also illustrated with the Danish "ghetto-package" mentioned earlier)? A basic principle for non-discrimination should be that support is distributed in tune with criteria inherently related to the nature of the support. What counts for social housing is housing needs. The use of a different criterion to decide who does or does not get access, identifying or privileging a real or a perceived "group" (skin color, ethnicity, religion, descent, language), is a form of discrimination. What if judicial authorities have declared the measure lawful? Those authorities may be right in their interpretation of current legislation. As a matter of fact, the Belgian anti-discrimination act includes language as a criterion, but there is not a single government body or agency assigned specific competence to evaluate its observance. Laws, or their enforcement, may themselves be discriminatory. Fortunately, they can also be changed. Multilingualism will remain.

Within the context of a multi-state organization such as the European Union (with 24 official languages), or of countries with more than one spatially identifiable major language community such as Belgium, Canada, Spain, or Switzerland, arguments can be made for a linguistic territoriality principle. To avoid the unfair dominance of one language over others, every language should be allowed to be "queen" somewhere. Note that this kind of privilege can befall only a few languages (in the case of the European Union, the 24 official ones, or a limited expansion of that range resulting from possible changes in local legislation) and that it cannot be enjoyed by the vast majority of the world's 6,000 languages. Nevertheless, such a principle would guarantee or facilitate, for the communities speaking the privileged languages, a serious manifestation of parity of esteem (a term often used in relation to identity politics, also when the parameters involved are non-linguistic, as in Northern Ireland).[23] In fact, some kind of linguistic territoriality regime is almost inevitably imposed in all states, which need regulations regarding the language(s) to be used in (publicly funded) education, in the provision of public services, in jurisprudence, in the distribution of administrative information, and the like. But the principle misses its communicative goals when Flemish road signs refuse to point a traveler to Liège or Mons because the Dutch names of these predominantly French-speaking cities is Luik and Bergen, or when a bomb alarm in a Flemish train station sounds in Dutch only. The road traveler's problem has become less acute thanks to GPS apps which fortunately do not care about language laws, and even the train traveler's predicament may find a solution in further developments of speech recognition and automatic translation technologies. But as long as access to such tools is not universal, there is a problem, easy to avoid and created solely by a counterproductive principle.

Territoriality principles (the defensible as well as the derailed), are built upon a distinction between languages that deserve political attention and tender public care (the *sublime*) and the ones that are seen mostly as a problem (a range of *ordinary tongues* spoken by people who do not easily fit into the imagined linguistic order). When European politicians praise mastery of foreign languages and are willing to invest in the education of "successful" multilinguals, they focus on the need to learn "modern languages," i.e., the economically profitable ones such as English, French, German, Spanish, and increasingly also Chinese. The sublime components of elitist multilingualism contrast sharply with the discouraged "home languages" mostly spoken by non-European immigrant communities, the ordinary and problematized multilinguals. These home languages include Arabic, even though, for instance in Brussels, it has overtaken Dutch as the second most common native language after French. Obviously, neoliberal marketability is involved in turning some languages and language communities into winners and others into losers.[24] But there is more.

The question of what to do with new forms of multilingualism, barring the dismal attempt to feign their non-existence, is not a simple one. Not all language communities are equally concerned about language maintenance. If language is everyone's property, protection is necessary, but everyone also has the right to renounce their rights. Concrete measures do not present themselves as a matter of fact, and a degree of creativity is called for. For instance, in the context of education. But it is precisely in that context that we can regularly see steps to restore the illusion of a simple monolingual orderliness, such as the cessation of experiments with bilingual or multilingual education. This has happened in a significant number of states in the

United States, a country that lends itself very well to comparative research on the achievement gap between native speakers of English and English learners. This comparison shows that the gap is wider in states with more restrictive language policies (cf. Gándara & Hopkins 2010). Alternative approaches, which give access to learning through pupils' primary languages at least part of the time while they are acquiring the dominant majority language, have been shown to be more effective (cf. Fillmore 1991). They are possible as soon as the demographic reality of an area shows a sufficient concentration of speakers of given minority languages. Extra efforts are then required. But they are worth the trouble – even from an economic point of view.

Immigrants, in general, adopt the dominant language of their new environment. They do so to different degrees and across generations, depending on context and needs. Any help they can get is more than welcome, and an open society is obliged to provide learning facilities. When this is done well, excellent results can even be witnessed in small rural communities, as in the case of Bosnian refugees acquiring Swedish (and its local dialects) in Swedish-speaking parts of Finland (cf. Ekberg & Östman 2020). This practical issue, however, tends to get muddled by ideology. In Finland, for instance, smooth integration may be hampered if immigrants arriving today are forced to first learn Finnish (the dominant language) even if they want to settle in Swedish-speaking areas.

The endlessly varying language landscape contrasts sharply with homogenizing thought. Not only language variation, but also the simplifying world view it is subjected to is supported by inevitable language processes. Ideologies do not lead an abstract life. They are sustained by language use that perpetuates implicit layers of meaning that are imperceptibly copy-pasted intertextually. That, also, is a natural process. We can, however, protect ourselves against the consequences. For instance, by sounding the alarm as soon as detrimental policies are presented as "normal."

One example of an ideological construct of what is normal is the differential treatment of languages that fit the paradigm of the successful modern bi- or multilingual inhabitant of the global marketplace versus the neglected but pervasively used everyday languages of sizeable immigrant communities. Very often, policies do not go entirely unquestioned. There is an awareness, for instance, that something should be done to accommodate Arabic in Brussels, where, as I mentioned, it is the second most common native language. In October 2016, a group of schools in Brussels announced their initiative, taken in collaboration with the Free University of Brussels, to start teaching Arabic. To ward off the expected protest, the announcement specified that this would be done only outside of regular class hours. This would make sense anyway to get kids from different schools together (while it would also make sense to let this count – still unimaginable in Belgium at this moment – as part of their regular education). But the argument that was counted on to win over the predictable opposition was this: Teaching Arabic in a secular environment would keep children out of the Koran schools. Thus, language policy meets the generalized suspicion of Islam. Even open-minded commentators, defending the initiative, bought the argument. Complicity does not have to be malicious. It may simply reside in the derailment of reflexivity: Reactions are expected (i.e., criticism of the initiative to teach Arabic), they are not faced head-on (e.g., by pointing at the importance of Arabic in Brussels today), but strategies are chosen to pre-emptively counter them by simply adopting their prejudicial premises (1. teaching Arabic is an added luxury that does not fit into the curriculum, and 2. there may be a link Arabic-Islam-radicalization). Putting derailed reflexivity back on track requires further reflexive steps, grounded in a refusal to be complicit.

Identity

I have used the term "identity politics" only once so far, and only in an explanatory phrase between brackets. There is a type of identity politics that is inevitable in any emancipatory process. Suffragette campaigns for women's rights to vote were not possible without pitting women (as an identifiably disadvantaged group) against men (the only ones who could even vote to give women voting rights). The right to strike had to be fought for as a measure to partly redress the power imbalance between factory owners and laborers – two identities embroiled in a political struggle. The Black Lives Matter movement is engaged in perfectly legitimate identity politics by protesting structural patterns of white privilege in the "Global North."

In the case of an anti-racist movement, the categories are rather vague (white vs. non-white). Also, "privilege" is a less tangible phenomenon than, say, the right to vote. No doubt it provides useful leverage to identify and correct historically grown inequalities. But it may at the same time be vulnerable to strategies of denial, and it may not always be sufficient to explain all types of contemporary experienced injustice. Anti-racism shares this vulnerability with the ongoing search for gender equality. Fortunately, many white people support anti-racist movements, just as many men support gender equality, but there is a tricky, hidden contradiction involved. Robin DiAngelo formulates this contradiction in her observation "that white people's moral objection to racism increases their resistance to acknowledging their complicity with it" (2018, p. 136). Escaping from complicity takes more healthy reflexivity and action than only the conviction that one looks at and treats everyone as an equal, without prejudice.

Identity politics "from below" is going to be needed for a long time. This prediction can be made because of its unfortunate co-existence with that other type of identity politics, the one pursued by dominant majorities. "Us" vs. "them" strategies, objectionable as they are in principle, cannot be avoided at certain times and places to achieve equality for the historically deprivileged. They can never be justified in the hands of the powers that be, using a clean "us" vs. "them" story to herd people into a nicely fenced political arena. Central to what worries me most in societal debates today is the complicit contention spreading among dominant majorities that strong emphasis on due respect for "us" does not imply a risk, however indirectly, of undue disregard for "them."

There are many shades of identity politics on the side of dominant majorities. What they share, however, is a sense of superiority and an exclusionary logic. These properties are sometimes openly admitted, sometimes flatly denied. Sometimes they are widely supported, sometimes hotly contested.

Just look at an historical example from the self-proclaimed champion of openness, liberty, and democracy, the United States of America. If you are American, you will remember Manifest Destiny. Manifest Destiny was the term used by journalist John L. O'Sullivan (in articles he published in 1839 and 1845) for his belief that the United States was destined to spread the democratic ideals of equality and personal freedom. The special virtues of the American people had set in motion the creation of superior institutions, in particular republican democracy, which would naturally proliferate and which the United States had the duty to share. This belief soon translated into the right to expand US territory. Ideologically supported expansionism led to the annexation of Texas, the war with Mexico over California, the agreement with Britain over the division of Oregon Country, and provided further backing for the numerous treaties pushing Native Americans into ever smaller pieces of land. There was no doubt a practical "need" to find living space for growing numbers of people. There was also a clearly racist angle: Even defenders of the notion of Manifest Destiny were against the annexation of all of Mexico because the Mexicans were viewed as inferior, probably unable to embrace all the benefits of American institutions, and (in contrast to the Native Americans) too numerous to be completely displaced.

This is an example of identity politics which clearly shaped the course of history, irrespective of the opposition it met (Whigs were opposed to the annexation of Texas though Texans themselves sought to join the United States), and irrespective of how far it may have deviated from mitigating formulations (O'Sullivan did not necessarily support expansion by force). As you must have noticed, there is not such a big jump from the racist angle of Manifest Destiny to the ideology of white supremacists today. And though white supremacy meets serious public condemnation, it still supports ideas – whether spoken out loud or simmering in the background – that make it difficult to eradicate systemic and institutional racism perpetuating historically established power relations in US society.

In present-day Europe, identity politics is all over. When practicing meta-politics, politicians know that a useful degree of simplicity will help them along. Since most of them are well-educated, however, they do not want to appear naïve. Therefore, they will generally acknowledge that people have multiple identities (as citizens of a country, as members of a family, as professional colleagues) and that populations do not have stable unique origins but have been formed by waves of migration. Still, national identity appears too convenient a rallying cry not to put it to political use. Nor was it left in the hands of a narrow circle of marginal politicians. Éric Besson, French Minister of Immigration, Integration, National Identity and Co-Development from 2009 to 2010 and Minister of Industry, Energy and Digital Economy from 2010 to 2012 under President Nicolas Sarkozy, devoted a book to it (Besson 2009). And so did Bart De Wever, probably the most powerful Flemish politician during the past decade (De Wever 2019).

Éric Besson, of French-Lebanese descent and born in Morocco, claims that precisely because of the different waves of people that have shaped French society, the French "nation" can only be the product of strong centralizing forces (*un pouvoir centralisateur*) that create unity by steering towards common values (*valeurs*). Central to those values is French laicism which guarantees a universalism that prevents fragmentation into competing identities (for instance, based on religion). This view, despite its many challengers,[25] seems to prevail politically. It was even the topic of an official national debate – without official conclusions – organized by President Sarkozy in 2009 after it had been a prominent theme in his 2007 campaign.

The French case certainly does not stand alone, though accentuations vary. I have already mentioned the Danish government's use of "Danishness" as an argument for homogenizing housing estates. Dutch election campaigns have become marked, from right to left, by an emphasis on "Dutchness." Nobody knows precisely what that means, but traits that have been foregrounded as "typically Dutch" include optimism and level-headedness, a healthy dose of curiosity and nerve, as well as an unrelenting attachment to freedom of speech and equal rights for all. This image allows Dutch Prime Minister Mark Rutte to talk repeatedly about the "common, normal Dutch people" (*gewone, normale Nederlanders*). In the UK, a liberal nationalism has developed which emphasizes Britishness, a national identity that remains abstract except for its reference to civic values and a strong focus on common language (cf. Adachi 2011).

It is a focus on language that takes center stage in the construction of a "national" identity in the Flemish part of Belgium, but it does not fill the entire picture. In all his writings on identity (from an earlier opinion piece to the more recent book I referred to), De Wever consistently distinguishes between a closed nationalism (emphasizing ethnocultural elements which cannot be acquired) and an inclusive nationalism based on civic and cultural elements that can be learned. In addition to the ideals of the Enlightenment, his prime example of a cultural element that can be acquired is "the language" (i.e., Dutch). De Wever also recognizes the contingent and variable nature of identity. He does not approach it as a goal in its own right, but as a legitimate tool, making use of people's basic social needs, to underscore the functioning of society. You will agree that it would be unjust to find fault in this positioning, as such.

Problems emerge, however, when the theoretical stance is translated into political practice. Thus, De Wever cannot resist fulminating against the decision of the Flemish Catholic schooling network to stop bending back on Catholicism and to provide facilities to its Islamic students. Though phrased in terms of their giving up their Catholic identity, his protest extends to calls upon Catholic schools to pay more attention to the teaching of Dutch, to education in "our values." I have already mentioned the relativization of racism by De Wevers's fellow party member Liesbeth Homans, then responsible for integration and equal opportunities, the testing area *par excellence* to find out whether it is inclusion or exclusion that prevails. And then there is the political decision-making on who gets in, and what happens to those who do.

Addressing those who want to get in, the Flemish government launched a brochure entitled *Migrating to Flanders: Starterskit* [sic] *for family migrants*. First, note the restriction to "family migrants." People who want to move to Flanders for other reasons than joining family members are not addressed. That does not mean no one else is welcome. Of course, expatriates needed for businesses and institutions are, but either it is assumed that they do not need a "starter's kit," or what the kit includes does not pertain to them. The brochure contains a lot of practical information in conjunction with implicit or explicit behavioral advice. Not surprisingly, the first requirement that is mentioned is "If you come to live in Flanders, you have to learn Dutch" – and this is re-emphasized six times (while few efforts would be made, if any, to enforce it upon high-ranking expatriates). The advice-giving is embedded in or interspersed with descriptions or suggestions of what is supposed to be typically Flemish, such as "Flemish people are punctual," or "Flemish people like peace and quiet." And many of the formulations reveal a slightly embarrassing expectation of deviant behavior: "It is forbidden to hurt someone mentally or physically, including your partner or children," "The government sometimes limits your personal freedom to make it easier for people to live together; the traffic rules are a clear example of this," or "Keep your home in a good state of repair." Even some rather basic ignorance is assumed, as in "Putting your signature to a document means that you agree to the contents of the document." And the overall tone is quite self-congratulatory: "No matter how different people are, in Flanders everyone is equal." If you know Flanders, you will agree that there is a lot to be self-congratulatory about, such as highly accessible and affordable outstanding education and topnotch health care. When reading *Migrating to Flanders* you may even find it quite welcoming, certainly if you contrast it with the explicitly discouraging messages that were distributed in 2015 and 2016 telling people NOT to come to Flanders during the so-called European refugee crisis. But the distance that is created between "us" and "them" is unmistakable.

The starter's kit is meant for those who are welcome, more specifically, those who have already been found entitled to a visa for reasons of family (re)unification. Since 2016, however, they are not allowed in, unless they sign a newcomer's declaration (*nieuwkomersverklaring*). Only part of this declaration pertains specifically to "newcomers": they must declare that they are willing to "integrate," that they understand that knowledge of "the local language" (idealized metonymically as the standard version of Dutch, even if this is *spoken* hardly anywhere) is essential for that purpose, and that they must become self-sufficient. Two-thirds of the declaration deal with obedience to the law, with a focus on human rights, freedom of speech, freedom of association, freedom of religion, freedom of sexual orientation, and equality between men and women. They must also declare that they understand that violence, threats, and terrorism are unacceptable. Useful and important as these legally enforceable principles are, one cannot stop wondering why not every Belgian citizen should be asked to sign a declaration to the effect that they understand all of this before they get the right to vote. Clearly, many "autochthons" are prone to infringements, which is why we need a judicial system. But if they violate rules, they simply misbehave (and can be punished), while a newcomer violating the same rules in the same way just does not belong.

Distance is maintained for those who manage to get in. At the peak of the refugee flow from Syria, Afghanistan, and Iraq, Flemish nationalist Theo Francken, State Secretary for Asylum and Migration, refused to handle more than 250 applications per day, leading to improvised camps in a Brussels park, depending completely on volunteer organizations for food and other necessities. Containment and discouragement seemed like the only policy goals.

Distancing, however, can also take subtler forms. Exclusion is now practiced under the façade of efforts at inclusion. In the Netherlands, two years after the introduction of an integration test (in 2003), the number of naturalizations had been reduced by half. Self-proclaimed inclusive nationalism in Flanders is the bedrock of a recent governmental policy statement (*Regeerakkoord, Vlaamse regering 2019–2024*) with sections on identity construction which clearly define everyone as outsiders who are not seen by the insiders as just like them. It is precisely this homogenizing integration concept which has aggravated interethnic and intercultural relationships in the past thirty years.[26]

What is wrong, you may ask, about a possibly honest attempt at self-confident positioning when political power must be translated into a plan for action? In fact, there have been many places and times in history in which nationalist movements were emancipatory. The Flemish movement is a case in point during a century-long fight for equality within the Belgian state structure – a fight, however, that seems too hard to stop after equality (and even dominance) has been achieved. Part of that history coincided with the strengthening of nationalist sentiments in Germany between the two world wars. Historical comparisons are always risky, but we should not let the extremism of genocidal Nazism obscure the fact that it was preceded, accompanied, and supported by moderate calls for self-confident nationalism, launched by possibly well-intentioned people, profiling themselves as open-minded intellectuals.

One such person was Friedrich Sieburg, a German journalist and author who had studied literature, philosophy, history, and economics. He presented himself explicitly as a progressive national socialist, and in 1932 he wrote an extensive plea for the protection and strengthening of German identity, *Es werde Deutschland* ("Becoming Germany"), that would appear in the year when Hitler gained power, 1933. Sieburg was a cosmopolitan mind, a Francophile, who had lived in Paris for years as a journalist, and he attached a lot of importance to the French translation of his book, *Défense du nationalisme allemand* ("Defense of German nationalism"), which also appeared in 1933.

In the preface to the translation, Sieburg expresses his desire to contribute to happy and peaceful neighborliness between France and Germany (*un voisinage heureux et pacifique entre la France et l'Allemagne*), and his wish to convince his French audience that what was happening at the time in Germany was necessary, i.e., the construction of a harmonious national image (*une image harmonieuse de son peuple* – something that in his view was evidently present in France but lacking in Germany). In a display of open-mindedness, he adds that he hopes the book will lead to numerous discussions, since discussion is the basis of human freedom and mutual understanding.

Far from exonerating Sieburg of his obvious complicity, there seems nothing reproachable in his overt motivations. But his defense of German nationalism, apart from the characterization of militarism as a basic and fundamentally innocent streak of the German people's nature (subjecting individuals to the collectivity without, in his view, being a threat to others), echoes many of the tenets of present-day identitarian discourse. Thus he rejects the (cultural) relativism which has made it difficult to discern the essence of the German character. His main point is that it is high time to develop common norms and values, a moral standard specific for Germany – it does not suffice to orient towards what others regard as useful or harmful, as good or bad. Anyone who does not break with hostile forces that do not fall into the established moral fold, is seen as a disturber of the peace. In other words, the German "us," just like any other form of national-cultural delineation, contrasts with "them."

In spite of the exclusionary implications of this stance, Sieburg can successfully parade as a benevolent, non-racist nationalist. In his book, he holds a plea against antisemitism, which is probably why it was banned in Germany in 1936. Yet the Nazi regime recruited him as propagandist in 1939, probably because he was able to hold such an eloquent plea for the necessity and inevitability of German nationalism, the creation of national self-confidence as ultimate resistance against runaway relativism. Briefly, without making claims about his intentions, Sieburg could not at all avoid being openly complicit in the havoc wrought by the Nazi regime.

Sieburg did not stand alone as a public figure whose ideas were put to use by Nazi Germany. A more prominent example may be Karl Haushofer, major general in the German army, military attaché to Tokyo in 1908–1910, World War I veteran, and professor of political geography in Munich from 1919 onwards. As a contribution to the regeneration of Germany, a hard-to-reproach goal shared with the Sieburgs of his day, he developed a theory of geopolitics in which he popularized the notion of *Lebensraum*, the dynamic (and therefore expandable) space needed by a nation as a living organism. This notion became one of the explicit ideological cornerstones of Nazi expansionism (just like Manifest Destiny had been for the American drive to the West), though Haushofer himself (like O'Sullivan before him) did not necessarily envision the use of military force. One of the victims of the violent expansion of German *Lebensraum*, the Austrian Jewish author Stefan Zweig, wrote about his encounter with Haushofer in India (when he was on the way to his Japanese mission), and about the admiration he developed for this man with his erudition and his genuine interest in Japanese language and culture. He had later read Haushofer's geopolitical work and even after World War II had already started, he had a hard time believing that it could have been intended to support aggressive expansionist politics (cf. Zweig 1944).

The exclusionary contour for Sieburg's national identity was clearly German. Though various present-day European nationalisms are partly restricted in similarly confined terms (French, Danish, Dutch, Flemish, to stick to the earlier examples), another ingredient is clearly situated at the level of a desired European identity. Thus, most moderate forms of national identity construction combine "local" properties (such as level-headedness for the Dutch) with a shared Christian (sometimes labeled Judeo-Christian) heritage, and norms and values that derive from modernity and the Enlightenment. That is why, despite professed freedom of religion, Islam is treated as a threat. In a more benign – though still distancing – approach, it is urged to "modernize," to develop into a "European Islam," as if inter-adaptation with the new local contexts is not already happening, applauded by some, contested by others, within as well as from the outside.

The construction of a national identity, whether or not it is conceived naïvely in essentialist terms or formulated with reference to ethno-symbolist theories of nationalism,[27] denies the very essence of "identity," people's right to define their own sense of belonging. It is not the case that people ever have full control to enjoy that right. We are, after all, heavily dependent on how others see us (as excellently illustrated by Rahier 2003). But rather than to simply identify what people have in common (which is often the overt goal), identitarian nationalism defines the contours within which the main question becomes "who has the right to belong to the nation?" The responses automatically lead to the exclusion of some, if not many. Nonetheless, the true task of a state should be to serve people living within its borders (which is the main sense in which borders can be said to be truly important), rather than to define who they are. A political ideology focused on national identity ignores that the central preoccupation of politics should not be the "nation," however defined, but rather the society that resides within (largely arbitrary) state boundaries. It is society that binds, without identifying, except at the level of citizenship, social security and solidarity, and a wide range of "codes," say legally binding norms of behavior (cf. Nancy 2010).

Identity, if taken seriously, is the individual's business to decide on the defining features one sees oneself as sharing with others. This is a simple recipe that contrasts sharply with the derailed reflexivity that is apparent in the proliferation of monitoring systems trying to measure degrees of integration (e.g., in terms of frequency of contacts between minority and majority members; cf. Schinkel 2013, 2018). Any qualification as "well integrated" will keep people outside, not only the not-so-well-integrated who are judged not to fit in – the very judgment that someone *does* "fit in" creates distance. The injunction to assimilate, euphemistically presented as integration, replaces as it were the old ties between church and state by a quasi-religiously endorsed link between the community defined in terms of national identity and the state. I agree with historian Marnix Beyen (2010) when, in line with the separation between state and church, he calls for a separation between state and identity.

From moderate forms of nationalism, including the ones that present themselves and may be intended as inclusive, there is a slippery slope towards overtly exclusionist versions. They may temporarily serve as dams against the extreme right. But dams can break. And keeping the dams weak must be judged as a form of complicity. The electorate may not be to blame for this. Usually, the choices they are given are limited, whether it is because of a petrified two-party system (as in the US) or because of a hopelessly convoluted fragmentation of the political landscape (as in many European countries). What is lacking is courage in the circles of political elites, concerned as they are with the meta-political considerations that guide their positioning. Rather than to confront exclusionary discourse, they cover it up by making it look reasonable. As a result, *what seems reasonable constantly moves in the direction of extremes.*

Masses can only be expected to slide in the direction of the center of gravity, the dominant trends. Again, it is hard to really blame them, especially after trends have turned into power structures. Individual expressions of disagreement can be costly. For Friedrich Sieburg, despite hypothetical hesitations, there may have been no way to resist being recruited into the Nazi propaganda machine. Even if Karl Haushofer did not intend his notion of *Lebensraum* to be abused for wars of expansion, he had no way of preventing them from happening; and probably he was not even free to try, since his own wife was of partly Sephardic Jewish origin and could only be saved from prosecution by the intervention of one of his students, Rudolf Hess, Deputy Führer from 1933 to 1941 – protection that ended when Hess flew/fled to Scotland on 10 May 1941. Similarly, Richard Strauss' connection with a Jewish daughter-in-law and half-Jewish grandchildren (as well as his cooperation with Stefan Zweig on the opera *Die schweigsame Frau*) must have made him a reluctant collaborator with the Nazi regime as first president of the *Reichsmusikkammer*. Less dramatically but equally revealing, Stefan Zweig (1944) describes how, with Nazi influence on the rise long before the Austrian *Anschluss*, some of his Salzburg friends started to turn away in the street in order not to be seen socializing with a Jew. All of these are examples from a period of political extremes, if there ever was one, but going against the tide always takes courage.

At the risk of sounding too repetitive, today much of the political agenda is dictated – though fortunately not controlled – by the extreme right. Moderate positions that are taken to curb migration, to confine diversity, and to define identity, are commonly conceived as weapons to hold back the radical versions of ethnic nationalism that we find in many political formations in Europe. But such moderate positions are fogged up mirror images of what, in the eyes of their proponents, they are meant to counter. What is worse, political parties of the extreme right are little more than the official faces of much wider undercurrents which they legitimize, implicitly if not explicitly.

It is hard to give these undercurrents (ranging from *PEGIDA* to *Génération identitaire*) a uniform characterization. To varying degrees and in varying ways they combine elements that are identitarian, xenophobic, anti-globalist, and anti-Islamic (cf. Zúquete 2018). Sometimes they are against the European Union, sometimes also anti-American. Many, however, rely on the idea of "Europe" as a basis for identity construction. They find a theoretical basis in Renaud Camus' (2011) "the great replacement" and work by other theoreticians of the New Right, such as Guillaume Faye and Alain de Benoist. Not all movements are equally combative, which is why some are getting banned, while others are permitted to continue their activities, though they often operate under the public radar. What they share is that they usually pit population groups against each other, sowing the seeds of violence, which sometimes germinate. "Sometimes" may be an understatement if we realize that in 2015 alone, and in Germany alone, there were nearly 1,000 incidents with violence against asylum seekers, nearly 100 of which were arson attacks on refugee shelters. In 2016 the incident figure rose to nearly ten per day. Whether we like it or not, this brings us back to where we started: Breivik's terror attacks in Oslo and on the island of Utøya. In the world view that drove him to action, he was not alone. The sympathy he knew he could count on means there was complicity.

Political respect

Panic has struck a significant portion of the card-carrying progressive intelligentsia. They are so afraid of being called "politically correct." The new normal that has been developing in the course of the past few decades, not only avails itself of the tool of utopic discourse in pursuit of national identity. The other side of the coin is the anti-discourse that you already saw illustrated as the relativization of racism and institutionalized distrust of anything looking or sounding Islamic. An equally important aspect of anti-discourse is the popular attack on political correctness. The foundational axiom of this attack: An invisible but powerful establishment polices language and thought to suppress inconvenient truths – it has made a range of ideas taboo. If attempts are made to lift the veil of invisibility, fingers are pointing in the direction of some media, but especially universities, which are presented as fortresses of a predominantly leftist intellectual elite, particularly in the humanities and social sciences.

The assailants form a mixed bunch of people. Anders Breivik devoted 27 pages of his infamous compendium to the cause, identifying the culprits as cultural Marxists and multiculturalists, and then spending hundreds of pages on his attempt to correct all the falsehoods that political correctness had infused into the European mind. Long before, supporting his own very different grounds for terrorist action, Theodore Kaczynski, aka the Unabomber, developed a line of argumentation that was more complex than Breivik's, but he blamed "leftism" for taking over the universities and, through political correctness, destroying the academic freedom they would have fought for tooth and nail, had they not been in control. A more scholarly master of the attack on political correctness is the already mentioned Canadian psychology professor Jordan Peterson, who situates it as a phenomenon at the extreme left which is dangerously polarizing society by reducing all speech and action to a power struggle between groups with distinct identities, ignoring the role and rights of the individual.[28] In the world of professional politics, the embodiment of the attack is Donald Trump, whose incessant mantra that he did not have time for political correctness (a term applied to just about all criticism of his policies) got him elected President of the United States as the one person who was finally speaking "the truth," as opposed to everyone else's "fake news."

None of these would want to be associated with each other. Breikvik, the anti-Islamic warrior for a new European order, and Kaszynski, the anti-technology anarchist, would not sympathize with each other's terrorist causes. Peterson would not sympathize with either, nor with Trump, since he says that he does not have eggs in the politically right basket. And Trump is just Trump. But what they share is their caricature of the left.

The term "political correctness," or "p.c.," has an interesting history. It first circulated in leftist circles only, ironically referring to excessive orthodoxy within their own ranks. By 1990 it had been picked up by conservative voices using it as a denunciatory term to ridicule the kinds of leftist orthodox excesses which would also be frowned upon by much of the left; a typical example to discredit so-called p.c. would be the request to eliminate courses in Western civilization because they would be inherently unfair to minorities and non-Westerners.[29] The term developed into an invective, expanding its scope to honest and valuable attempts to fight sexism, racism, xenophobia, and homophobia, which (i) point at their structural foundations in traditional male dominance, in a white sense of superiority, in nationalistic reflexes, and in heteronormativity, and which (ii) suggest that inequities do not correspond to a "natural" order of things and that, therefore, we should all be mindful of speech and action, discourse and practice, supporting the idea that they do. Conservative forces and the political right uphold a grotesque caricature of these positions as inherently obstructing free research and speech, making it impossible to tell "the truth."

Is free speech really being obstructed? You have inevitably noticed that anti-p.c. voices can be heard all over (all the way up to the White House, not so long ago) and that they form the substance of international bestsellers. Their being silenced is no more than a figment of the imagination. Yet, fear of such accusations, and forgetful of the intrinsic value of the progressive positions under attack (a value that may very well explain their widespread dominance in academia), a significant portion of the self-declared progressive side of society has been dragged along into the anti-p.c. camp. Just a faint-hearted lack of courage parading – and possibly intended – as the honest pursuit of truth? Or an unambiguous case of complicity?

Progressive positions go too far if they censor alternatives. But hardly anything can be wrong with their adamant defense. Jordan Peterson accuses "the left" of reducing social dynamics to power struggles between groups with defined identities. He is right that ultimately the entire cause of equal treatment and equal opportunities must be situated at the level of the individual. But members of minority groups are consistently denied the right to be approached as individuals; they are seen and treated as members of those groups. When an African American young man in an American city steps out into the street, he knows that he is more likely to be suspected of criminal behavior, to be stopped by the police, maybe even to be shot at, than his white neighbor.[30] A young man of North African descent in a European city will more easily run into passport control than his autochthonous friends. Anyone whose native language is not Dutch in a Flemish city, knows that he or she will constantly be seen and judged as an "other-lingual." And a woman looking into the mirror in the morning is likely to see herself as a woman, while a man has the privilege of just looking at himself as a human being. Privilege is what it all comes down to. And *privilege is rarely seen by the privileged.*[31] Which is why the Petersons of this world can make such a fuss about the primordiality of the individual – a position which I fundamentally support, but without losing sight of the groupness into which so many individuals are compressed who would much prefer to be treated as individuals as well. Too many are denied that privilege by being looked at as part of a collectivity. This is the foundation of historically grown racism. Thus, the fight for group rights – identity politics indeed – becomes inevitable, a dreadful instrument to achieve a goal that fundamentally has nothing to do with group identity, but that will be needed so long as equal opportunities remain a neoliberal myth rather than to be a reality. Group formation is a completely natural process, but it should be the individual's right to decide what group(s) s/he wants to belong to.

Some forms of what is called political correctness are easy to ridicule because they may, indeed, be practiced with undue diligence. Favorite targets have been "trigger warnings" and "safe spaces," treating students (in anti-p.c. terminology) as "snowflakes." It may not be necessary to systematically warn students whenever something possibly shocking is coming up in readings or course materials. It may not even be possible in all cases. Graphic depictions of sexual violence are an easy case, but what about subtle forms of moral cruelty? Some contend that it may not even have the desired anxiety-reducing effect for the people coping with specific traumas for whom the warnings are intended (such as victims of rape who are, unfortunately, not such a marginal group). But there is nothing wrong with the idea, and trying never hurts, as long as it does not lead to facile avoidance of what is unpleasant. Trigger warnings are now common fare in news broadcasts. I have not heard complaints about news anchors warning their audience that images to be shown can be disturbing. Nor is the practice of rating films for "parental guidance" disputed; even Netflix issues content warnings.

You will probably agree that sheltering students from the realities of the cruel outside world is not the smartest idea. But though some so-called safe spaces may have been so conceived, generalizing such a characterization is, again, a caricature. The basic idea is not so different from what used to be called special-interest discussion groups sharing experiences of marginalization or the pursuit of a common goal. These may be derogatorily called "echo chambers," but they do serve a useful purpose and lead to insights one might not be able to reach alone. The primordial example of a safe space is probably the AA meeting (and, by extension, the group therapy session), where individuals are free to express themselves in the knowledge that they will not be judged. Infantilization – which you will agree must be avoided – is only inevitable in the minds of the privileged and of those devoted to the fight against a phantomized political correctness.

Another area liable to easy dismissal is lexical hygiene. There is no reason why abandoning the generic use of the personal pronoun "he" could automatically be expected to reduce male dominance in society. After all, gender equality is not necessarily stronger among speakers of languages that do not distinguish between male and female in the third person singular, such as Finnish or Hungarian. But that does not mean that consciously using "she" instead of "he," or the stylistically convoluted "s/he, "he/she," "he or she" does not serve a purpose. It is an attempt to keep awareness of, and to transcend, an unwanted pattern of dominance. The decision of the French authorities to abandon the distinction between *Madame* and *Mademoiselle* is a valid attempt to step away from the outdated implications of a woman's marital status. Similarly, there is nothing laughable about a railroad company changing the form of address in its public announcements from "Ladies and Gentlemen" to "Dear passenger" to include all those who do not recognize themselves in the prevailing gender duality. Or, to use another example, there are excellent reasons to bury the dichotomy between autochthons and allochthons (the popular "us" vs. "them" distinction in Belgium and the Netherlands), simply because it unduly categorizes a significant segment of the population as not really belonging where they live (and, increasingly, where they have been born). Or, to say it with McConnell-Ginet (2020), *words matter.*

Extending this reasoning from word choice to cultural traditions, it is a good thing that (again in Belgium and the Netherlands) the colonial stereotype of the black servant is being abandoned in a popular children's festivity.[32] This is a necessary form of accommodation to people's sensitivities. There are equally good reasons to produce revised versions of children's stories, as is done in countries like Sweden, if the original reinforces unwanted stereotypes and role patterns. The originals will become quite interesting data for historical research, especially the history of ideas.

The democratically organized decent treatment of (members of) groups of people is more important than the names we give them. It is an illusion to think that changing language changes reality. We should not forget that the categorizations that go hand in hand with naming practices will always blur members' individuality, no matter what the names are. Still, linguistic choices are important, as naming practices may reproduce and keep discriminatory images alive.[33]

An interesting test case emerged recently in the Dutch-speaking world, where the white population, being the absolute majority, is in the comfortable position not normally to be obliged to think about itself in racial terms. The traditional racial adjective for "white" is *blank* in Dutch. This is a color term meaning "white," but it is used mainly for skin color, and it carries connotations of purity when applied to other phenomena such as wood, metal, sand. The more general term for white, less restricted in usage, is *wit*. Anti-racist movements have pointed at what they perceive as a terminological asymmetry: Because the opposite of "black" (*zwart*) is not just the equally general *wit*, white people are somehow "special." Minority members have therefore started to use the color term *wit* instead of *blank*. This has led to white anti-p.c. comments arguing that now an identity is being forced upon whites (at least those who would like to keep calling themselves *blank*), just like white racists force identities upon others. Ironically, letting people know what this feels like, may have been precisely the one good reason to intervene with traditional usage. So long as that extra reflection does not seep through, however, the move is not successful.

Does this mean that white people refusing to call themselves *wit* are racists? Of course, too much attention to specifics of language use – in whatever direction – robs the link between forms and meanings of their essential dynamics and negotiability. It may lead to counterproductive self-censorship or the unreasonable shaming of those who happen to use the wrong words. It is all a matter of finding the proper balance, but above all, keeping the debate going. For this, it is important to "stay woke" – another one of those terms that are magnets for anti-p.c. ridicule.

Freedom of speech, the desire and the right to express one's thoughts in pursuit of truth, is a valuable commodity. But even if you are radically against any form of censorship (including, perhaps, anti-negationism laws), I hope you do not object to the following two propositions.

The first proposition is that freedom of speech also includes the freedom to investigate speech and to critically comment on it. Research will inevitably reveal frames of interpretation which form the substance of underlying ide-ologies (cf. Verschueren 2012). Some frames of interpretation may be more beneficial than others; some may be outright dangerous. In any democratic society it must be possible to point this out, to debate the implications, and to advocate action accordingly. We all know that the metaphor of the "war on terror" supported (if not led to) decades of actual war and turmoil, while 9/11 could also have been framed – horrible as it was – as a crime for which the culprits had to be pursued and brought to justice. We also know that talk-ing about migration as an invasion or a tsunami, about immigrants as scum, about protesters as trash to be neutralized with a high-pressure cleaner, about people without valid residence papers as a swarm of illegals, about male ref-ugees as testosterone bombs, about refugees in general as a peaceful-looking Trojan horse ready to attack from inside, is not going to lead to harmonious integration policies. These discursive framings (none of them invented) are not innocent, and fighting them is legitimate. Silence is complicity.

A second proposition is that efforts should be made not to let free speech go beyond decency. This is more troublesome. Free speech involves the right to offend. But people also have a right not to be offended or harmed. Sensitivities differ, and not everything can be captured in laws. So, it is an open question of how far one can go. What complicates the issue, moreover, is the fine line between humor and offence. A money-grabbing stereotype of Jews paraded at carnival will predictably be followed by protest, and it is completely legitimate to demand an apology, even if it was "just for fun" and even if the designers of the float are barely aware of the associations triggered by racist depictions nearly identical to those in Nazi Germany. I hope you agree that it is better to avoid senseless abuse. Similarly, while freedom of speech can be called upon to produce an individual "Mohammed cartoon" to satirically make a point, launching a Mohammed cartoon competition (as proposed by Dutch extreme-right politician Geert Wilders in September 2018) is a dubiously provocative gesture, to say the least. And what to do with attention-seeking pundits who claim that jihadism is in essence more malicious and dangerous than Nazism was, without taking into account what emotional reactions this could trigger for victims of the Holocaust – leaving aside the historical validity of this claim?

Does this mean that behavior must be adjusted to every form of sensitivity? The charge of cultural appropriation, for instance, is a tough one. Do we have to go along with every form of protest against someone's use of others' hairstyle or dress code? Where is the boundary between appropriation and cultural borrowing, one of the common processes in cultural change? Human cultural development is so fast and strong precisely because of its cumulative potential. If people feel offended, it would be wrong to simply dismiss their feelings. Any feeling of offense deserves being openly addressed, debated. But that also means the outcome remains debatable and cannot be pre-given. Thoughtless borrowing of other people's cultural symbols can be quite disrespectful. At the same time, we must not forget that charges of cultural appropriation run the risk of being trapped in essentialism, a basic ingredient of harmful identitarian thought.

Similarly, what about the charge of intrusion you may encounter if you want to write about women, homosexuals, or minorities while you are a man, a heterosexual, or a white majority member? Where is the boundary between transgression and empathy, an attempt to understand, the very basis for building a society? These issues must be kept in clear focus to avoid a so-called "cancel culture," even if that term is itself mostly used to stop short of serious reflection. Clearly, the "sensitivity readers" employed by publishing houses to avoid publishing materials that are in any way offensive, have a job in which derailed reflexivity looms large. But a difficult exercise is not an impossible one.

Respect is the bottom line. And since it concerns relations in the public sphere, let us call it *political respect*. There is a relationship with tolerance. But tolerance implies power difference and is mainly an attitude from the stronger towards the weaker.[34] Respect is simply what everyone is entitled to, in every direction. It is incompatible with any sense of superiority, or any systematic stereotyping or stigmatization of the "Other."

This position may evoke the specter of cultural relativism. Remember Sieburg, who thought that too much relativism had prevented the development of a strong German identity. He was still looking at the level of individual "nations" and could easily imagine an equally valuable French identity side by side with the German. Today, identitarian movements in Europe and North America combine the nationalist stance with a belief in the absolute superiority of the enlightened culture of modernity. They forget a few things. One is the dark side of modernity and the use of its weapons of rationality and efficiency at the service of worldwide colonial power as well as local forms of totalitarianism on the left as well as on the right.[35] Are these, perhaps, the kinds of excesses strategically forgotten because they are secretly longed for? It would be unwise to regard all this as part of a faraway history. The same dark lines continue straight into the easy rationalization of forms of violence of which we do not see the consequences; think of "surgical" drone strikes; also in the past, violence became easier the more systematic, industrialized, and distant it became. That has not changed.

A second point of neglect in the glorification of Enlightenment and modernity is the wide and ever-changing range of grey areas it engenders. Enlightened principles do not necessarily lead to the superior position of complete clarity. A plea for the primacy of reason is justified by the need to seek the truth. Freedom of speech should help us approach the truth by making it possible to voice and balance opposing views. But how is truth served if freedom of speech is used to willfully voice blatant falsehoods, as happens so often in public life? Should we be resigned to the rationality of the folk wisdom that a rumor is not true until it has been officially denied? Are we not free to condemn (even on the basis of legislation specifically designed for that purpose) the freedom to distort and lie in ways that can harm people? Reason, as the ultimate instrument to reach the truth, is also invoked as an antidote to dogma and tradition. But isn't much nationalist identity construction, while appealing to a sense of superiority based on Enlightenment values, justified precisely in terms of history and tradition?

A third point, almost completely overlooked, is the naïve belief in the universality of reason, independent of experiences. Related to this, there is arrogance in the belief that all those wonderful inclinations to rely on reason, empiricism, and objectivity, are entirely "ours." We may want to avoid the idea of "multiple modernities," if only because the term may suggest the possibility of juxtaposing separate and homogeneous civilizational entities with their own deep-rooted cultural programs. But the underlying idea that there are different ways in which societies can be organized around principles of individual self-determination and rationality, is certainly valid. Even in the European and North American cradle of these principles, they have at least given rise to "successive modernities," i.e., constantly changing shapes of and institutional transformations in capitalism and liberal democracy, sometimes clearly showing progress but not without places and periods of regress.[36] One of the particularities of European modernity may even be its stress on permanent transformation.[37] Let us also not forget that human reason is inherently fallible.

Does the recognition of a dark side, of grey areas and contradictions, and of the flawed universal ambitions of modernization, or the acceptance of cultural diversity, lead to unqualified acceptance of cultural relativism? Is everything cultural of equal value, as the caricature of a relativist stance (as evoked by Bloom as early as 1987) would have it? We already asked that same question earlier in this essay. The answer is still the same: By no means.

Political respect requires a perpetual balancing act between two primordial principles: Fundamental openness to diversity, and complete equality at the level of the individual. Some aspects of equality can be legislated, but much will be left to the realm of interpretation. Openness to diversity means, then, that everyone must be accepted as an equal partner in debates about interpretations. This requires a readiness to question what seems self-evident, because the assumptions all of us live by may not be the only valuable ones – they may differ depending on one's socio-cultural or socio-economic background. Some interpretations will inevitably prevail over others – and may eventually find their way into legislation. But all of this is an ongoing process in which freedom of speech, practiced with respect, is a foundational asset. Dogma cannot be allowed to dictate any course of action. This is why worldly power cannot coincide with religious belief, though on many issues religious belief may come in, to feed debate. Political respect, therefore, is enlightened and modern, but only from the vantage point of modernity as a never-ending flow of rational, multi-party, interactional decision-making that must be fully contextualized to the extent that, if need be, it allows for emotion and tradition. A balancing act indeed, for which we all share responsibility.

Solidarity

The true locus of diversity is the individual. The argument of which this is a basic premise, however, is not at all individualistic. On the contrary, it entails a strong plea for solidarity (cf. Wilkinson & Pickett 2009 or Sennett 2012). Probably the main duty that derives directly from human rights – everyone's (individual!) right to a life in human dignity, with food, shelter, education, health care, access to justice – is the obligation to behave in a solidary, rather than a solitary, way. This is more important than voluntaristic altruism.

Just like respect, solidarity is reciprocal. That means it is in everyone's interest, as anyone may need and reap the benefits at some time. *Solidarity is self-interest without being selfish.*

Solidarity is not just an attitude. It involves the democratically organized sharing and (re)distribution of material and immaterial resources. It must, therefore, be developed and implemented at the level of political entities. These entities may be local, sub-national, national, or supra-national. Politically organized solidarity may, of course, be supplemented with informal initiatives that emerge spontaneously within networks that transcend territorial limitations (by being more local or more global) or that involve commitments with variable temporal dimensions (from momentary to indefinite). This is what the idea of the "commons" is based on, from community gardening to the digital commons of Wikipedia. Many communities worldwide have developed local forms and concepts of communal work and mutual support that fit into this paradigm: From East African self-help events (*harambee*) and the Indonesian ethos of sociality (*gotong-royong*, the "joint bearing of burdens"), to the task-oriented gathering of friends and neighbors in Finland (*talkoot*) or Norway (*dugnad*).

You may be tempted to assume that such informal forms of solidarity gain importance with increased mobility (sometimes perceived as an increase in diversity). Maybe they do, as an extension of what used to be very local traditions, for the simple reason that there is a tendency to underscore solidarity with loyalty towards a group one belongs to. True solidarity, however, must go beyond in-groups, and can be truly effective only when feelings of shared fate get generalized. Therefore, it is politics, governments, that must provide the stable core of solidarity to guarantee that everyone can benefit from inevitably limited resources. And this can only work well with an enlightened politics that does not define the polity in identitarian terms.

Despite the social origins of some nationalisms, an interesting bond has developed between nationalist yearnings and (neo)liberalism. Against the background of the myth of the free market and the fetish of economic growth, regional autonomy (or even independence) is advocated to "localize" responsibility, effectively eroding mechanisms of solidarity, in a drive for efficiency. It is often seen as democratic to avoid transfers of means to those who are judged not to behave responsibly. In broad strokes, this is what happened in the European Union when Greece was down and out after the banking crisis of 2008. The attitude was extended beyond the economic, and worldwide, when COVID-19 made governments scramble for protective gear, ventilators, and medication, even at each other's expense in those difficult months in early 2020. A similar lack of solidarity is manifesting itself in COVID-19 vaccination programs which may not even reach parts of Africa, Asia, and Latin America in 2021.

Solidarity is undermined by nationalist reflexes, but not only in the relationship between nations. The same happens within state boundaries. Identitarian nationalism does not allow everyone within state boundaries to "belong." Solidarity is restricted to a vaguely delineated but seemingly clear intuitive group. This undermines democracy as an essential space for diversity. Acquiescing in this state of affairs, the normalization or "mainstreaming" of what should be defiantly protested as extreme and unacceptable, is certainly complicity.

Lack of solidarity extends into every walk of life which politicians, meta-politically mindful of their party's market value (and their own possible expiration date), have allowed to be fully regulated by a neoliberal logic. There is the often-heard argument that countries with more liberal governments (in the neo-sense) are "doing better" than others. What else can one expect if the rules of the game by which performance is measured are liberal? It is disappointing to see how even socialist and social-democratic parties have eagerly followed the so-called "third way," in practice the neoliberal way, and that they have systematically allowed rightist populism to dictate the political tone and agenda, notwithstanding their lip service to more noble goals. Complicity, no doubt.

It would be unfair to solely blame politicians. Even the outspoken enemies of big capital, the consumer organizations, eagerly compared banking products with an eye to maximal gain for their clients. Only the biggest profit was good enough. It was not important, before the crash, where the surplus came from, or what virtual monetary flows it was based on. Free market mechanisms are unflinchingly promoted for necessary resources that should be in public hands, such as energy and, pretty soon one should fear, water. And all of us, we grab the best buys, from electronic gadgets to clothes, knowing very well that for every cheap product someone pays, with sweat if not with money. Complicity again.

You will have noticed that I am using complicity as just another word for shared responsibility. Even if you and I cannot *be held responsible*, we cannot throw off the scent of our meandering choices. We may have been – or felt – forced into a course of action. We may not have seen alternatives. Sometimes we have no doubt been willfully blind. Turning a blind eye to the ruling and harmful vigor of meta-political action may have seemed like an easy way out. Fighting gravity takes an effort. Especially if you, like me, have enjoyed a healthy dose of privilege, there is no excuse for abandoning the fight, for not resisting the comforting complicity of silence. For, unless you believe in grander schemes, the meaning of life is life itself; life is just a cruel joke for those who get no chances; and those are, sad to say, vastly outnumbering us.

But change is possible. And we all share the responsibility to bring it about. How can we resist? How can we act? There is no uniform answer to such questions, as there are many different kinds and degrees of complicity, from guilty collaboration to mere acquiescence, requiring different types of action and resistance. But one rule is clear. If you are in a privileged position, the opposite of actively exploiting privilege is not its non-exploitation; it must be an active contribution to counter privilege. Or, as Ibram X. Kendi

(2019) would say, specifically focusing on racial privilege, the opposite of racism is not non-racism; it can only be anti-racism. Moreover, "A racist or antiracist is not who we are, but what we are doing in the moment" (Kendi in *The Guardian*, 6 December 2018). More will have to be said later about possibilities for action. But first we make a small detour, following the thread of derailed reflexivity through an educational institution, the university, and the media.

Notes

1 See www.start.umd.edu/gtd/ (last consulted 27 December 2016).
2 Source: www.vpc.org/studies/driveby2010.pdf.
3 The Australian-born shooter at the Christchurch, New Zealand, mosques on 15 March 2019 posted a manifesto entitled *The Great Replacement*, echoing Renaud Camus (2011), to explain and justify his actions.
4 From a letter addressed to the New York Times in June 1995.
5 When adding functions to the names of politicians, these always relate to the period in which the reported facts or events are to be situated.
6 Breivik's compendium, p. 1436, refers to Sarkozy, Merkel, Cameron, "who have all admitted that multiculturalism has been a failure and a disaster for Europe."
7 The term was first introduced by Steven Vertovec (2007) when correctly pointing out that the group-based policies of modern Western states (with the UK as an example) were not conceptually equipped to deal with the type of demographic complexity that characterized the reality of its social diversity.
8 Reference is to a controversial "foreigner law" that was passed by the Belgian federal parliament on Thursday 9 February 2017.
9 The use of the terms "autochthon" (referring to the "local" population) and "allochthon" (referring to people with a migration background) is widespread in The Netherlands and Belgium.
10 "Politics at a meta-level" is different from what "meta-politics" – which I will nevertheless use as a short-hand equivalent – sometimes means in analyses of political communication. For instance, Jan Zienkowski & Benjamin De Cleen (2017) use the term to describe attempts to reconfigure the meaning of politics itself and the relationships between capital, government, civil society, and citizens. This is still fundamentally political, and it deserves the "meta" label only because of the attempt to create a different level of politics, an attempt to change the range of available political options (a usage which has been in circulation in various alternative circles trying to escape from traditional political dichotomies such as left and right, and not uncommonly in circles of the extreme right which describe themselves as metapolitical movements – think e.g., of Alt-right – because they operate outside political parties; cf. Maly 2019). My use of metapolitics designates a political move away from what, in my opinion, should be the truly political (in quite a normative and traditional sense). It is also distinct, therefore, from Badiou's (1998) usage in which metapolitics is proposed as a philosophical alternative to political philosophy by relating philosophically to politics under conditions of politics.
11 A brilliant little book explaining how this strategy may explain the victory of the not-so-eloquent George W. Bush over the much more cerebral Al Gore is Silverstein (2003).

12 Populism is a mixed bag. There is not only the likes of Donald Trump in the US and Jair Bolsonaro in Brazil; in Europe the spectrum goes from the radical right (with its many manifestations from Geert Wilders in the Netherlands to Heinz-Christian Strache in Austria) to movements incorporating strongly leftist positions (e.g., Beppe Grillo's Five Star Movement in Italy). It is not unusual to find competing populisms within the same polity. For a more detailed account of populism, you should turn to Jan-Werner Müller (2016). For a short introduction, see Cas Mudde & Cristobal Rovira Kaltwasser (2017). For the difference between populism and nationalism and an example of transnational populism, see De Cleen et al. (2019).

13 The culture of fear is what sociolinguists have recently been analyzing as processes of *insecuritization*, the discursive spread to people's everyday concerns of perceived threats to national security. See Ben Rampton & Constadina Charalambous (2020).

14 For successful examples see James Fishkin's "deliberative polling" method (https://cdd.stanford.edu/what-is-deliberative-polling/). For further advocacy of horizontal political models, see, e.g., Graeber (2013).

15 Note that I steer away from a cognitivist approach in the "cognitive science" sense that heavily gravitates towards computational and neurophysiological reductionism. I consciously adopt Vygotsky's (1978) notion of "mind-in-society," rejecting the commonly accepted implicit dualism. For insightful discussions of what is at stake, see Watson & Coulter (2008).

16 Reference is to Harjit Singh Sajjan, the first Sikh to become Minister of National Defense in Canada, assuming office in November 2015.

17 Cf. Dominique Charpin, "Immigrés, réfugiés et déportés en Mésopotamie dans la première moitié du deuxième millénaire av. J.-C.," lecture delivered at the Collège de France, Paris, 13 October 2016.

18 For an extensive study of how "race realism" creeps into academia, see Angela Saini (2019). Popular references for believers in the relationship between race and IQ are the 1960's works of physicist William Shockley and educational psychologist Arthur Jensen, but especially Richard Herrnstein & Charles Murray (1994), though the authors of *The Bell Curve* are mostly interested in achievement gaps about which they do not claim they can be attributed to genes, allowing as much of a role for environmental factors.

19 See Peterson's discussion with Stefan Molyneux at www.youtube.com/watch?v =iF8F7tjmy_U).

20 This is literally what *Vlaams Belang* politician Filip De Winter said a week before the May 2014 elections in Belgium: "Het probleem is niet de vergrijzing maar de verbruining" ("The problem [of this society] is not its greying [= its ageing population] but its browning").

21 "Other-lingual" is a direct translation of the Dutch word *anderstalige*, which is commonly used especially in Flemish political discourse to identify speakers of other languages as a social problem to be addressed.

22 For classical examples of how unnoticed aspects of style, such as differences in intonation patterns, lead to misunderstandings, see, e.g., John Gumperz (1982).

23 A vocal and convincing advocate of the linguistic territoriality principle as a matter of parity of esteem, is the Belgian philosopher Philippe Van Parijs (2014). To read more about parity of esteem as a principle for democratic post-conflict identity politics as in Northern Ireland, see Robin Wilson & Thomas Hennessey

(1997). For a sociolinguistic discussion of the relation between linguistic diversity and social justice, see Piller (2016).

24 For good examples of the competitive marketing of languages, see Luisa Martín Rojo & Alfonso Del Percio (eds.) (2019). For a general critical account of the relations between language and capitalism, with tentacles into colonialism, see Heller & McElhinny (2017).

25 In addition to Jean-Luc Nancy and Nasser Demiati, whose work I refer to elsewhere in this essay, among the numerous challengers of the political idea of a French national identity, it is worth mentioning Esther Benbassa (2012), François Jullien (2010), Hervé Le Bras (2017), and Michel Wieviorka (2020). On 4 December 2009, some 20 social science researchers published an opinion piece in *Libération*, entitled "Nous exigeons la suppression du ministère de l'identité nationale et de l'immigration" ("We demand the dismantlement of the ministry for national identity and immigration").

26 For a lengthy analysis of the homogenizing integration concept in the early 1990s, see Blommaert & Verschueren (1992) and (1998).

27 Critics of nationalism usually rely on the work of Benedict Anderson (1983), Ernest Gellner (1997), and Eric Hobsbawm (1990). In varying ways, these three scholars counter the essentialist reflex which much nationalism is based on, arguing that nations are largely invented and relatively recent phenomena. In a defense of nationalism, reference is usually made to the ethno-symbolist theories of John A. Armstrong (1982) and Anthony D. Smith (2009). The central thesis of ethno-symbolism is that complexes of narratives, symbols, and attitudinal factors were unifying forces for (ethnic) group identities long before the birth of the nation-state, and that the "inventions" of modern nationalism were often based on pre-existent ingredients.

28 See for instance the *Munk Debate on Political Correctness,* 24 May 2018, available at www.youtube.com/watch?v=MNjYSns0op0 (last consulted on 31 March 2020).

29 The date 1990 is somewhat random, of course. But this was the year in which an influential, trend-setting article was published: Richard Bernstein, "The rising hegemony of the politically correct," *The New York Times,* 28 October 1990, Section 4, p. 1, https://nyti.ms/29uUBPH (last consulted on 1 April 2020). 1990 was also the year of publication of Roger Kimball's *Tenured Radicals.* Kimball develops an extensive plea against the politicization of the humanities and what he sees as the imposition of a radical agenda which makes civil debate impossible about issues such as affirmative action or homosexuality.

30 Unfortunately, there is a reason for the Black Lives Matter movement, triggered by the shooting of Trayvon Martin on 26 February 2012 in Sanford, Florida, but unable to prevent similar incidents (most infamously the shooting of Michael Brown on 9 August 2014 in Ferguson, Missouri, and George Floyd's death by suffocation at the hands of a police officer on 25 May 2020 in Minneapolis, Minnesota).

31 For this reason, Eddo-Lodge (2018) decided it was no longer useful to talk to white people about race. Clearly, she still does (hence the book), but the message does not leave anything to the imagination.

32 I am referring to "Sinterklaas," a traditional children's day involving lots of presents that are sneaked into the house by Sinterklaas, a saint in bishop's garb, with the help of his servant "Black Peter." The Black Peter figure, depicted as the colonial stereotype of the black African (as black as possible, with curly hair

and thick lips), has been the topic of heated controversy for many years. A form of accommodation has been reached by turning the servant into a figure with black sooty stripes on the face, the logical result of the fact that the pathway for sneaking presents into the house is the chimney..

33 This is one of the reasons why responsibility has become an explicit theme in discourse studies (cf. Östman & Solin eds. 2016).

34 Tolerance or "toleration" can also be used in a multi-directional sense, as is done in some of the contributions to Mendus & Edwards (eds.) (1987). The reciprocity that is demanded for respect is, of course, also completely in line with Popper's (1987) argument that toleration does not have to tolerate attempts to put an end to toleration.

35 As early as 1944, Horkheimer and Adorno developed their theory of totalitarian regimes as one of the consequences of the Enlightenment's rationalization of humanity. Later, in 1989, Zygmunt Bauman linked modernity to the holocaust – in a much more sophisticated way than I can summarize here – by explaining that the more rationally one can explain action, the easier it is to cause suffering. Already in his preface, he says, "*The Holocaust was born and executed in our modern rational society, at the high stage of our civilization and at the peak of human cultural achievement, and for this reason it is a problem of that society, civilization, and culture.*" (p. x)

36 To read up on the notion of multiple modernities, see Shmuel N. Eisenstadt (ed.) (2002). For a lengthy discussion of the issues involved, including the notion of successive modernities, see Peter Wagner (2012). For the plurality of democracies, see, e.g., Voltmer (2013).

37 This point is made in Bjørn Thomassen's (2012) anthropological critique of the multiple modernities paradigm, which also figures concepts such as parallel, global, manifold, alternative, competing, repressed, fragile, reflexive modernities, as well as counter-modernities.

2   At the university

My comments on society, succinctly captured with labels such as meta-politics and derailed reflexivity, can be read as a lengthy footnote to Hartmut Rosa's verdict on present-day politics:

> In late-modern politics, it is no longer (if it ever was) the force of the better argument which decides on future policies, but the power of resentments, gut-feelings, suggestive metaphors and images. Images no doubt are faster than words, let alone arguments, they exert instant, if largely non-conscious, effects. The better argument becomes powerless in the face of dynamic waves of opinion-formation.
>
> (Rosa 2013, pp. 56–57)

It would seem, therefore, that there is an urgent need to replace the civilizational zeal of political power brokers by reinvigorated emphasis on education. Civilizing is what European powers wanted to do in their colonies, and it is the process we want to subject anyone to who does not seamlessly fit into our societies, newly perceived as (too) diverse. It only serves a narrowly conceived modernity, functioning too easily as an instrument of domination.

By contrast, education should aim at freedom, autonomy, insight, and responsibility. It serves a more universal conception of human progress in equality. The tools for education, ideally leading to more firmly reflective positioning beyond a politics of opinion, should be found, if anywhere, at our universities, the temples of research and training from which well-informed awareness of social structures and processes should spread across the entire path of educational growth and into the most diverse corners of public life. But does not the way in which I am formulating this sound suspiciously close to the leftist agenda about which the anti-p.c. brigade claims that it already dominates the universities? Lo and behold, the university itself is not untouched by what is happening elsewhere in society. Continuing with Rosa:

DOI: 10.4324/9781003206354-2

Now, it is almost self-evident that the formulation, filtering and collective weighting of arguments is a time-consuming process. This is true for the world of science, where one might well argue that the speed and succession of conferences and papers is so high and, much worse, the number of papers, books and journals published is so excessive that those who write and talk in "publish-or-perish"-Age hardly find sufficient time to develop their arguments properly whereas those who read and listen are lost in a host of repetitive and half-baked publications and presentations. I am firmly convinced that, at least in the Social Sciences and the Humanities, there is, at present, hardly a common deliberation about the convincing force of better arguments, but rather a non-controllable, mad run and rush for more publications, conferences and research-projects the success of which is based on network-structures rather than argumentational force.

(Rosa 2013, p. 55)

All academics are familiar with this problem. At the drop of a hat, motions (sometimes lamentations) are written, circulated, and signed to try and convince the powers that be to let universities return to their core business: Research, research-based training, and research-based service. Well-informed books and position papers have been written (e.g., Donoghue 2008, Collini 2012, De Dijn et al. 2016), critical (and sometimes quite amusing) analyses have appeared (e.g., Chamayou 2009, Gill 2016), and even manifestoes have seen the light (e.g., The Slow Science Academy 2010, DORA 2012). Notwithstanding this general awareness, and sporadic (usually shy, sometimes outspoken and courageous) attempts at moving in a different direction, universities have been fully imbued with the model of a production economy – ironically at a time when their less tangible quest for insight should be all the more valued in light of a so-called knowledge economy. How does this work? What is the problem? Why should we care? More specifically, should you care at all if universities are far removed from your daily preoccupations?

Winners and losers

Neoliberalism as the root of all evil (to paraphrase Monbiot 2016) is no doubt a hyperbolic idea in need of nuance. As argued earlier, however, derailed reflexivity is one of its byproducts, affecting domains beyond the economic by generalizing the focus on competition. Some successful businessmen who look beyond economics, also see that market values have "penetrated into areas where they did not properly belong" and that they have "undermined professional values" (Soros 2019, p. 74). Competition requires winners and losers, and therefore monitoring and assessment. This is the source of the managerialism which has been hovering over all segments of university life for several decades. Before presenting yet another analysis of this trend, let us remind ourselves briefly, and somewhat naïvely, of what universities are for – an exercise undertaken at greater length by many others, much earlier, and from many different perspectives.[1]

Quoting Clark Kerr on developments he observed in higher education from 1963 to 2001, the period between his first and his last formulation of *The Uses of the University*, "Higher education is more market-oriented—the student market, the research market, the service market" (2001, p. 192). These three "markets" constitute, not surprisingly, the core areas of academic responsibility. Kerr adds,

> But there should be more to a university than that. Specific actual markets do not express all the needs of society for university attention. Some such non-market needs are training for good citizenship, advancing cultural interests and capabilities of graduates, providing critiques of society (we hope from a scholarly perspective), and supporting scholarship that has no early, if ever, monetary returns.
>
> (2001, pp. 192–193)

This modification, however, presupposes acceptance of the marketability of research, research-based teaching, and research-based service. It is precisely this idea that must be questioned, as it does not follow naturally from the presumption that there is usually some kind of competitiveness between human beings. Academic work does not need to be transformed into market shares – the calculable amount of research money spent and the measurable "output," the sheer number of students one can attract, or the visible display of findings offered for public consumption. Research must be carried out in pursuit of answers to interesting and potentially important questions; it is the never-ending quest for understanding and clarity, the reduction (never the elimination) of uncertainty. Teaching is aimed at insight, whether pure or applicable; it passes on knowledge, it nurses the desire to pursue "truth," and it provides the training needed for such endeavors. Service must be provided to shed light on questions the non-university public lives with, or to contribute to research-based solutions to problems it faces. None of these areas can flourish without freedom of action, within margins set exclusively by social needs, cognitive abilities, ethical concerns, and "material" feasibility. All of them require maximal cooperation. Marketability is anathema.

It is easy to see where the university's market orientation is coming from. The most benevolent interpretation is that the comparative measurement of efficiency and productivity is necessary to guarantee optimal use of funds, especially in countries where higher education is largely dependent on government financing. You will agree that universities must be accountable for their use of public funding. But only the "corporate" university, with its clients, partners, and stakeholders, reduces accountability to the best-practices governance that merely balances financial cost and economic benefit, with special care devoted to the "valorization" of research.

The way in which accountability is now approached goes back to a long history of bureaucratization as a process characterizing the "modern" or rational design of organizations. As sociologists have amply shown, organizational or institutional practices are in tune with managerial ideologies.[2] Selznick's opening line in his classical study of the Tennessee Valley Authority as a democratic planning organization for the management of the production and distribution of fertilizer and electric power immediately gives us a quick look at the central issue: "Whatever the ultimate outcome, it is evident that modern society has already moved rather far into the age of control" (1949, p. 3). Organizations require planning. Planning requires control. In an organizational context, whether in a public institution or in a private company, control always involves the delicate interplay between lines of authority and the behavior of individuals. The most effective control mechanisms, whether organized democratically or in an authoritarian – if not totalitarian – manner, are those in which formal authority achieves stability and legitimacy by coopting the different strata of active individuals into the leadership. When this is done successfully, in Selznick's words, "what is shared is the responsibility for power rather than power itself" (1949, p. 14).

Agreement on managerial principles translates power into bureaucratic processes. Principles must be agreed upon, and, ideally, they should be in tune with the *raison d'être* of the type of institution or organization in which they are expected to operate. What is happening to universities, however, is the appearance of managerial principles that do not come from within but are imposed from the outside, derived directly from a neoliberal ideology which gives center stage to markets and competition conceptualized in terms of measurable cost and output. A focus on measurement and competition – which can also be seen to develop on the basis of a different logic outside of the liberal capitalist world, as for instance in China – does not even come close to what universities are for. But the managerialism could not work without the coopting processes just mentioned. This means we will eventually also have to touch the topic of complicity.

It is also easy to see what the university's market orientation leads to. In February 2020, universities in the UK started a massive strike action, the third in three years. There were a number of practical grievances addressed by the University and College Union (UCU), all of them related to diminished esteem for higher education, which, in a market logic and in spite of high tuition fees (and the resulting unaffordable student loans), is largely parasitical on the "real" economy: Declining salary scales (and even pay inequality), inadequate pension plans, serious job insecurity (lots of casual part-time contracts), and rising workloads (resulting from the hunt for ever more money-generating students without adjustments to the size of academic staffs). At a deeper level, poor working conditions resulting from the market economics applied to the universities stand in the way of excellent research, devoted teaching, and commitment to service. Only honest passion can explain that excellence, devotion, and commitment survive, despite recent developments.

The example of the UK may be an extreme consequence of years of Thatcherism and the resulting New Public Management tradition.[3] The situation is not as bleak everywhere, but the basic problem is widespread. A worsening student/faculty ratio is common fare, and so is the shrinking size of a core faculty in combination with a growing periphery of cheaper part-time and temporary teaching appointments. Outcomes are measured in relation to salaried time – an institutional use of the clock in keeping with the organized work discipline of industrial capitalism. Often a clear "business" goal is lacking so that "each cut in spending is simply a springboard to the next" (Lorenz 2012, p. 606). Fundamentally, all of this fits Rosa's diagnosis of "a natural consequence of the competitively driven acceleration-game" (2013, p. 75) which is bound to lead to alienation "Each time we 'voluntarily' do what we do *not really want to do*" (2013, p. 83).

What is it, you may wonder, that academics do "voluntarily" that they do not really want to do? Let me try to formulate my own succinct analysis, maybe just adding a somewhat idiosyncratic angle to what has already been described extensively by others (and to what is commonly discussed during academic coffee breaks – when there is still time for those). Before starting, however, I must immediately clarify that not all people in the academic world are engaged in doing things they "do not really want to do." Winners usually do not object to the rules of the game they are playing.

An academic cytokine storm

In the good old days – I hope you do not miss the irony – access to academic positions was often highly dependent on networks and nepotism. Exceptionally, there were even (patrilineal) academic dynasties. Inbreeding within universities was not uncommon – though practices differed significantly from country to country (with, it must be said, an extremely healthy resistance to the hiring of one's own students at the better American universities). Academic rank was sometimes more dependent on age than on achievement. This is not the kind of organizational practice you would like to return to. A healthy dose of meritocracy is no doubt useful. Some systematic reflection and evaluation may guard against quality problems, just like cytokines are important to fight infections. But when the body's immune system overreacts, cytokines go into overdrive and attack the entire body, sometimes causing death. In academia, *evaluative reflexivity and meritocracy have completely derailed*, causing nothing less than a life-threatening cytokine storm.

The storm which academics "voluntarily" enter when following their passion into the university system is only marginally related to what they really want to do. However, they cannot "sit it out," as it rages through the academic career from beginning to end. They have no choice, so it seems, but to fight the elements that cross their path. Some may be interested in status, though societal esteem for a university position has already greatly diminished. About the majority willing to devote their lives to academic work, we may safely assume that they are really interested in the pursuit and sharing of knowledge.

Most do not enter the system naïvely. When they start their PhD research, they know that this does not guarantee an academic job. They also know that countable criteria stand between them and their doctorate. At the better universities, their trajectory mainly includes essential graduate-level training in their field, in addition to a dissertation. At many institutions, however, points must be collected along a number of dimensions that distract from the concentrated pursuit of answers to specific research questions. The simple reason is that the production of many more doctorates than can be absorbed into the academic world is accepted as a fact of life, and it is regarded as responsible policy to make sure that the new doctors have skills other than those directly related to their research, so that they can still fit into the labor market. Not surprisingly, therefore, highly valued types of meta-level training include the acquisition of management skills. Often there is also a requirement to publish (or to produce work accepted for publication) before defending the doctorate – a strange feedback loop from expectation patterns further along the academic career path which will be open to only a minority.

After obtaining the doctorate, the game turns into top-class sportsmanship. Without countable items on one's CV (such as a few serious publications – the one or two "required" at some universities may not be enough), a PhD degree rarely leads to a postdoctoral position. Other types of academic appointment are, more often than not, part-time and/or without prospects of tenure.

Only the lucky ones, a minority amongst those who have already been playing the competition game with complete devotion, end up in tenure track positions. One would assume that after being hired competitively on the basis of quite explicit job descriptions and after a rigorous screening process, young academics can then fully and passionately engage with the tasks at hand. The managerial logic, however, does not allow so simple a trajectory. More often than not, the chosen ones are first subject to an amicable discussion of objectives to be pursued, formulated in terms of measurable output (a number of publications, an amount of research money to be accumulated, doctorates to be produced) within a specified time span. Participants involved in this process are invariably reasonable human beings, but the threat is always there that at the time of evaluation, a mismatch between the objectives (signed in writing) and the real outcomes will mean the end of a career. No space is allowed for the uncertainty that is probably the most fundamental ingredient of any truly scientific endeavor. From that point onward, the maze of bureaucracy unfolds endlessly.

When I first wrote this text, I tried to capture the many lines of (derailed) reflexivity that collectively represent the bureaucratic maze of current academic life in a simple graphic. The result always looked too simplistic. What follows, therefore, is simply a narrative hinged on a few action categories: Real academic work (the job), preparation, evaluation, measurement, and parasitic activities. Just keep them in mind as anchoring points as you read along. You may also want to jump to the next section if you are an academic, in which case the content of the following pages will be highly predictable for you.

Unlike in an ordinary organizational context, especially in any self-respecting area of industry, only the most luxurious appointments in academia come along with the provision of the means to do **the job** one is hired for. *Service* is not an issue; apart from institution-internal service (chairing committees and taking part in other aspects of the bureaucracy), that is the most noncommittal part of the job anyway and can be filled in (mostly) at will; though public visibility is appreciated, it is rarely the object of evaluation, let alone measurement. For *teaching*, students, lecture rooms, a library, and (where needed) laboratories are provided, and involvement in *program development* is more fun than it is burdensome (unless one takes the lead). But both service and teaching must be research-based, turning *research* into the most centrally demanding task. Precisely at that level, a major hurdle must be taken.

Most research requires funds. Funds are not (or very sparingly) provided directly by the university. The lucky appointee, therefore, must immediately develop a strategy to start competing for research money, both within the university and from outside (national and international) sources. In pursuit of cash, a significant amount of time must be invested in the **preparation** of *grant proposals*. The best strategy, already involving a form of derailed reflexivity or academic life at a meta-level, is to write a proposal for research that has already been (partly) carried out. Because this reduces or eliminates the uncertainty of serious research, you can show clearly that you know what you are talking about, and you can be relatively certain of the output, which allows you to use part of the acquired funds to start the research on which your next proposal is going to be based. Unless the work at a meta-level is extremely successful so that reserves are built up, one side effect of this process is that there are never means available to address issues immediately at the time when they become pertinent. Grant proposals take time, and so does their evaluation, which itself usually precedes the availability of funds by many months. Consider the problem of a social scientist who wants to address the lived experiences of people while the COVID-19 pandemic unfolds in the first months of 2020. Those experiences cannot be reproduced at a later time, when only some so-called objective indicators may still be traceable. Yet understanding them may be important for addressing comparable events later.

No one doubts the usefulness of **evaluation**. *Student evaluations* of teaching performance can provide important feedback. Usually, however, elaborate systems are set up, as bureaucratic instruments of control, with questionnaires that provide quantifiable results fed into tools for sophisticated statistical analysis. Most of the time, the results of all this effort are put to rest, only to be obligatorily revived and referred to at pre-ordained moments of staff evaluation. Only rarely do they reveal problems that were not already known. But the logic of the corporate HR paradigm must be followed.

Peer reviews are an essential ingredient of the publication process. With increasing pressure to publish and a corresponding expansion of publication channels, probably more energy goes into this than is warranted by purely academic concerns (most academics probably receiving more requests for reviewing tasks than they can properly carry out), but there is no acceptable way to avoid it altogether. Some smart businesspeople are offering paid-for peer reviewing (usually in combination with other services such as English language editing) to help authors prepare their manuscripts before submission to a journal.

Similarly, the reviewing work of *funding committees* is inevitable. It could, however, be greatly reduced if the means to do academic work would come with academic appointments. Granted that a certain degree of competition for specific means could still be useful, there is no way to justify, even in purely economic terms, the amount of time and energy that goes into the work for funding agencies. Consider a moderately attractive European grants program aimed at 10 projects but drawing the attention of 100 teams. Imagine that each of the teams consists of four people, each of whom spends two weeks on the preparation of the team's proposal. This moderate estimate of time investment means that the mere preparation of proposals for this one program takes 16 years of work, only 1.6 of which will lead to research funding. But there is more involved. Each proposal must be read and reviewed by at least three people. Even if the reviewing of a serious proposal takes only half a day, this involves another 150 days of work. Add to this the expenditure for the staff of the funding agency, for maintenance of its infrastructure, for travel and accommodation of a more restricted committee that meets for the final decisions, and it is clear that the awarded grants have to be extremely generous to warrant the time and money already spent before any of the funded research can even start.

Mind you, there are certainly lines of research for which competitive funding schemes can be justified, particularly to stimulate directions of investigation of special importance to society. But with generalized competition, without the stable availability of basic means to do research in the area one has been hired for, the only result is an ever-widening gap between winners and losers. Also, the generalized practice of project-based research financing is one way of controlling *what* research is done (not only in areas that deserve to be stimulated), a violation of academic freedom which is detrimental to progress in (other potentially important) areas that happen to fall outside the (partly fortuitous) scope of the funding organisms. The preparation of research, both topically and methodologically, is directly affected by calls for proposals and by expectations about evaluation criteria and procedures.

In principle, the layer of evaluation, barring excessive managerialism and competitivity, constitutes an important manifestation of reflexivity. A serious problem comes up, however, at the level of **measurement** which feeds into the actual practice of evaluation and therefore also into the (preparation of) real academic work. It is part of the bureaucratic logic that evaluation must be based on objectively recorded data. This may seem like a matter of elementary fairness. It allows you to calculate your "value" in the academic marketplace and to plan its "growth." But it is only necessary because of the competition game: Measurable facts facilitate comparison. That is why criteria enter, such as the amount of money competitively obtained for research, the number of doctorates produced, the number of publications (further measured in terms of the ranking of journals and the frequency of citation), appearances for keynote lectures at conferences, and – when teaching is concerned – even the attractiveness of one's courses in terms of class size. All of these are only tangentially related to quality, if at all. Their pernicious effect – where reflexivity derails – is that not only is evaluation based on them, but that, precisely for that reason, they effectively *change academic behavior*, the core of what universities are for. Uniform measures induce uniformity of behavior and may result in mediocrity, disguised as professionalization.

What pays off is to maximize chances of publication by conforming to expectations, avoidance of anything that is too controversial or too atypical. What pays off is to carefully choose channels of publication in view of bibliometrically established impact factors and rankings. What pays off is to multiply publications, whether by fragmenting one's findings or by forming alliances with other researchers – if three authors each write three articles, and all three have their names on each article, each author ends up with nine publications – or by acting as co-author of what is written by one's students. Specifically, it is useful to boost one's own ranking by creating citation networks. What pays off is not to let doctoral students define their own paths, but to assign strictly circumscribed tasks to them which can certainly be met within a specified time period. Since the production of doctorates "counts," more research money tends to go to doctoral students than to postdoctoral positions. A disproportionate amount of research is therefore carried out at the pre-doctoral level which, in combination with the pressure to get results within a limited amount of time, reduces the average level of innovativeness. What pays off is jumping on popular themes and juggling with fashionable concepts. Thus, themes are addressed, and concepts are handled not because of scientific considerations but merely because of their assumed persuasiveness. An example of a meta-process, if there ever was one. What pays off, finally, is to use all these achievements in the writing of new grant proposals.

As a special piece of advice, especially younger scholars should wisely leave behind all "non-productive" work that does not augment their measurable competitive capital. This includes devoting time to teaching, thinking up risky and unpublishable ideas, writing books, and (in the non-English-speaking world) writing in other languages than English. Strangely enough, it also includes spending time on the activities without which measurement would not have anything to base itself on, such as reviewing for journals and editorial work. Against this background, it is mildly surprising that scientific fraud does not occur more often.

This is not, unfortunately, where the story ends. Inside the universities, administrative overheads have been growing rapidly, advertising budgets follow the felt need for inter-university competition, and "professionalization" activities must ensure that all academic staff members get their noses in the right direction to maximize the institution's market share. As a true expression of market thinking, a vast layer of (often profitable) **parasitic activities** has engrafted itself onto the academic world. The demand for measurement has created an impressive *benchmarking industry* which carries the competitive logic to the level of inter-university rankings at a national and international level (cf. Hazelkorn 2015). In addition to dozens of local rankings, there are a few "authoritative" international ones: The *Times Higher Education World University Rankings (THE)*, the Shanghai Jiao Tong *Academic Ranking of World Universities* (*ARWU*, the so-called "Shanghai ranking"), and *QS Top Universities* (or *QS World University Rankings*, produced by Quacquarelli Symonds Ltd since 2010, after initial collaboration with *THE* from 2004 to 2009). It is bad for a university's reputation not to be in the top 200 of at least one, preferably more, of those (i.e., roughly the top 1.1% of the world's university-level institutions, estimated at over 18,000).

Ranking, which itself has become a business, is based on indicators measuring academic performance. Since only attributes can be used for which internationally comparable data are available, the indicators are invariably limited to areas related to measurable research output (such as citation indexes, Thomson Reuters' "Web of Science" data, search results on Google Scholar, numbers of Nobel Prize winners) or to reputation (established on the basis of surveys or measures such as the G-factor, i.e., the number of links to a university from other university sites in Google's search engine data). In a sense, *THE*, *ARWU*, and *QS* are the Standard & Poor's, Moody's, and Fitch Ratings of the academic world. Just like the three big credit rating bureaus, they create a virtual discursive reality which practices must conform to in order to remain viable. It is not unusual for university administrators to nudge their academic staff to respond positively to requests for participation in *THE* or *QS* data gathering for their rankings. The questions which professors get to answer, however, mainly boil down to a popularity poll.

Benchmarking goes far beyond these ranking ventures. In the context of the European Union, for instance, a European Center for Strategic Management of Universities (ESMU) was set up as early as 1986. When it organized a conference on "Benchmarking in European Higher Education" in 2010, it did not leave anything to the imagination:

> In its recent **Europe 2020 strategy**, the European Commission emphasized the need to enhance the performance and international attractiveness of Europe's higher education institutions. HEIs need modern management tools to foster institutional reforms, improve their operational efficiency and strengthen their capacity for innovative change in the face of rising global competition. The Commission itself has explicitly underlined the crucial role of benchmarking in optimizing university activities and educational outcomes.[4]

Performance, attractiveness, management, reform, operational efficiency, innovative change, global competition, benchmarking, and optimization of activities and outcomes – it is all there and captures complete acceptance of the managerial ideology of measurable competitiveness. A follow-up conference in 2011 summarized the main concerns in its title, "Facing the rankings: Using benchmarking tools for strategic positioning," for which invitations were sent out, accompanied by a pdf of a benchmarking hand-book (ESMU 2010). The handbook itself was the product of a second two-year project, indicative of the amount of energy that goes into peripheral activities, and – since a handbook is meant to be used, especially when funded by a policy-making body – foreboding an avalanche of further benchmarking endeavors.

The avalanche sweeps along everyone and everything on its path. Professors with management duties or ambitions have to learn the tricks of the trade, which is why they are invited to executive leadership and man-agement workshops (usually led by non-academic consultants who have found a lucrative market), and why wholesale parasitic conferences – not just training workshops – are held to "engage in the modernization agenda," whether or not specifically targeting identified levels of the academic hier-archy, such as provosts or deans. The rank and file can only hope, mostly in vain, that when their actual or would-be leaders return to base, they have not picked up too many "useful" ideas carrying along extra administrative concerns for everyone in times to come, or that they will not "encourage" everyone to go on an academic leadership journey of their own to be taught how to do better time management and how to inspire members of their teams to enhance their performance.

Actually, multi-day "boot camps" for professors are getting organized by professional consulting agencies, at a cost. Publishers thrive on self-help books on academic leadership; a random Google search gives you dozens of hits. Further expanding the circle of parasitic activities, companies have been set up for *grant proposal training*. In the best tradition of the lobbying industry, they have familiarized themselves thoroughly with the practices of funding agencies, on the basis of which they provide invaluable advice. One of the main skills is to understand a funding agency's priorities (of which the contextual embedding may be more important than the textual formula-tion), and especially how to fit research into pre-defined categories. This is not a trivial matter. Inevitably it affects the orientation of one's research.

Another necessary skill is versatility in the project management vocabu-lary which provides the scaffolding for lengthy research calls and guidelines (cf. Giles 2005). As a researcher, you should not just know your field of expertise, but you'd better know how to convince non-experts of its impor-tance, you'd better know how to develop a project concept in response to a work program topic (or "call"), you'd better know how to predict impact (preferably beyond the academic realm) in a way your evaluators will believe, how to describe exploitation issues and risk assessment and monitoring, how to put together a sound project budget, how to prepare for audits, how to design a work plan with work packages presented in a convincing implementation table, how to define deliverables and key performance indicators (or KPIs). Conversely, you can never assume that the managers attaching their seal of approval to your project are expected to understand your field of expertise. Briefly, you should learn not to assume that quality, accountability, transparency, professionalism, flexibility, and the like, can be interpreted as the corresponding words in natural language (cf. Lorenz 2012).

Similarly, the bigger scientific publishing companies provide *publication training* at academic conferences, usually with an emphasis on how to get into their own journals. *Media training* is offered to help academics increase the public visibility of their research. And yes, there are the *predatory journals* and even *predatory conferences* trying to lure the inexperienced, under pressure as they are to get their first trophies in the competition game. Young academics without well-established networks, but eager to find their way in a highly competitive environment, can easily be exploited this way.

Totalitarianism light

If, in Thomas Aquinas' categorization, my own complicity in relation to the broader societal issues has been to remain more silent than I could have, in relation to the academic world it has been my own direct participation. During my career, I have been fully involved in publishing, conferencing, chasing research funds, and supervising doctoral students. I was lucky enough, though, to be able to start doing this at a time when it was appreciated and rewarded while its quantification did not hang above our heads like a sword of Damocles. Like so many of my colleagues I have witnessed gradual changes in the direction of the current predicaments which we have not been able to avert. This inability must be taken literally. Many of us have commented and protested, but to no avail. Personally, I served my faculty as dean for eight years, in a crucial period of this development. Observing the ever-expanding circle of procedures, controls, and quantification models, I regularly tried to get a simple rule adopted at the higher echelons of my university: Whenever a new procedure is launched that clearly aggravates the non-academic burden on the academic staff, it must be shown to replace or simplify others. This never worked. Not even when it was proposed as an interesting "benchmark." The irony was only mildly appreciated.

The process responsible for the fact that developments could not be stopped against the wishes of most of those concerned, is quite transparent.

It is a mild form of totalitarianism (cf. Lorenz 2012). The first ingredient is the generalized competitiveness, with an evaluation and surveillance craze, institutionalized distrust, which makes everyone watch everybody else. The second is directly produced by the first, while further enabling it: An incorporation of the imposed norms, and their active (even honest) defense by those who stand to gain. The third and probably most lethal aspect is the hierarchical structure which obfuscates the precise locus of power. Who really imposes the norms? At every level of the hierarchy (e.g., a faculty), those in charge (e.g., deans) encourage everyone within their authority to play the competition game as skillfully as possible; if not everyone plays the individual ranking game, everyone loses collectively, because the entities they belong to (whether it is the faculty, the department, or the research group) are compared with similar entities, and this comparing is done at a higher level of the hierarchy (i.e., the university) with the power to distribute means. At the level of the university, responsibility for the norms is waived (while their observance is carefully administrated) on the grounds that everyone else is supposed to accept them and not playing by the same rules would mean relinquishing competition for the means distributed at yet a higher level (e.g., government and funding agencies).

The bottom line is financing, especially in countries where always the same means are (re)distributed among the same competitors. This is not only the case in small countries like Belgium, but also in the bigger ones such as the UK, where the regular Research Assessment Exercises (RAE, renamed Research Excellence Framework, REF) are dreaded, disputed, but ultimately bowed to (with gentle nudging from the school's RAE/REF manager). No one seems to have any real choice, since the system has teeth: Money can be given or withheld. Complicity makes the difference between having a job in academia or not having one. In other words, *complicity can be bought*. Accepting the format means losing freedom; rejecting the format means marginalizing oneself. As in most totalitarian contexts, the loss of freedom is taken more lightly than the risk of marginalization.

Maybe you have no affinity with the university. You may be inclined to regard it as an elitist institution far removed from real life. There are good reasons for such a view from the outside. The argument I am trying to make is that its distance from real life is aggravated by its having imbued the neoliberal views and practices of the surrounding society, which has integrated it into a shady world of meta-level activities. Pressure to publish, and publish fast, is harmful to the care with which research is carried out and reported.[5] Society is the victim. All of us suffer if vital knowledge fails to be obtained and communicated. On the other hand, academic administrators are so concerned about reputation management that they use all possible means to project an image of social responsibility, even when pertinent issues do not come up. Perhaps this is just erring on the side of caution. But a curious mix of involvement and estrangement clouds the academic horizon.

Is this an irreversible process? It is not all trouble and affliction. Yes, the search for research funds, sometimes in response to open demands to aim for "self-financing," has steered some researchers into open complicity with companies that do not serve concerns about health or environment,[6] or with the think tanks of disreputable political movements. It has silenced academic criticism of industrial sponsors as well as some political regimes. In general, however, social responsibilities are taken very seriously. Yet, the energy to make positive contributions, particularly with an eye to the acquisition and spread of knowledge useful in the fight against the gravitational forces of derailing reflexivity, cannot be fully unleashed without an escape from those forces in the first place. No doubt unionization could work, but only with a "union" willing to question all the premises of current practice – a thoroughly subversive attitude and genuine resistance. One can try, possibly even succeed.

Why is it important to try? Because research and education are crucial to turn the tide of socio-political processes that threaten to undermine the foundations of democracy. But they can hardly do so effectively, so long as they share the premises that turn the wheels of the current societal and political machinery. If universities take themselves seriously, they should rid themselves of those premises. They should set an example by putting the consequences of a radical paradigm shift into practice. That will give them the authority to address the foundations of wider social and political problems. Comfortably wallowing in a resigned inability to do so is an extreme form of complicity. Society deserves better.

A similar story can be told about the media. There, however, I position myself as a consumer, observer, and researcher, rather than an active participant.

Notes

1   See, for a small but representative sample, John Henry Newman (1852), Clark Kerr (2001 [1963]), Henry Rosovsky (1990), Marc Bousquet (2008), Frank Donoghue (2008), Martha Nussbaum (2010), Stefan Collini (2012).

2   I am very grateful to Rod Watson for reminding me of the classical literature on this topic, starting from Weber's (1922) notion of *Zweckrationalität*, goal-oriented rationality (distinct from, but also occurring in combination with, value-oriented rationality), as the basis of bureaucratic organization. How institutional practices developed in conjunction with managerial ideologies in society at large and in industrial contexts was further explored most notably in Selznick (1949), Bendix (1974), and Beynon (1984).

3   For an analysis of how the so-called New Public Management affected public services in general in the UK, and health care services in particular, see Ferlie

et al. (1996). For an application to universities, see Lorenz (2012). For specific implications to British universities, Head (2011).

4   Quoted from the announcement of the conference that was due to take place on 11 June 2010 in Brussels, signed by ESMU President Frans van Vught (www.p edagog.uw.edu.pl/fckeditor/userfiles/file/Conference_EBI-II_Letter.pdf).

5   On 6 July 2020, just a few months after the coronavirus pandemic took off, Retraction Watch (https://retractionwatch.com) already reported 22 retractions of published COVID-19 papers or posted preprints. The database of Retraction Watch reaches 1,400 retractions per year. But this only bears on articles in which mistakes have been detected grave enough to warrant withdrawal after publication.

6   A sad example is to be found in the complicity involved in consciously biased research supporting the pharmaceutical industry (cf. Angell 2005 and 2009).

3   Through the media

Education plays a crucial role in the preservation of public and political sanity. So do the media. Both, however, suffer from the afflictions of the societies which they serve. Both, we may add, have the responsibility to rise above the constraints that keep them from concentrating on the contributions they could and should make. Universities in liberal democracies mimic the organizational contours and directives of their societies. Not only does this stand in the way of a critical attitude towards such organizational patterns, the nature of the patterns themselves, revolving around too much attention to meta-level activities, diverts institutions of higher education from their central mission. Thus, they risk sub-optimal functioning, if not failure – which is bound to have an effect at all levels of education. Can we see similar things to go wrong for the media? If so, where and how?

To begin with, a quick comparison with the health care sector. Neoliberal organization reduces efficiency to "cost efficiency," i.e., a ratio between input and output, rather than aim for effectiveness in view of a specific goal. During the COVID-19 crisis in 2020 and well into 2021, it has become clear (for those willing to see), that the over-efficient neoliberal structuring of the health care sector in many countries has depleted the extra capacity that was needed to meet a real crisis: Personnel, stocks of protective gear, intensive-care equipment such as ventilators, even hospital beds. This was realized with a shock. The shock was big enough to prompt drastic action so that the worst scenes, such as the army trucks transporting coffins in Italy's Bergamo or corpses lying around in the streets of Ecuador's city of Guayaquil, could be avoided in most places. Whether it will have been big enough to lead to lasting corrections after the crisis, remains to be seen. If we want to be sure, nothing less than a revolution in organizational logic (and political priorities) will be needed.

What has been happening with the media is almost exactly the same. A failure to deliver in the media, however, is felt less dramatically than in the

DOI: 10.4324/9781003206354-3

health care sector. Therefore, there may be less potential for correction. Let me explain.

The information funnel

In the public domains of higher education and health care – at least in societies where these are predominantly "public" – the obsession with cost efficiency is driven by an essentially legitimate concern with accountability for what is done with the taxpayer's money. The main paradigm shift that is needed in those areas – moving away from the dominant neoliberal road we have been traveling for decades – is to look at expenses less as a burden and more as an investment for the common good. This would allow for serious long-term thinking and planning. The media, however, are predominantly private in most parts of the democratic world, so that the terms of efficiency tend to be dictated by the potential for relatively short-term financial gain for shareholders.

There are still important public service broadcasters such as the BBC, but even those depend to a significant degree on commercial activities,[1] and they must increasingly compete with companies, the vast majority of which belong to a limited number of gigantic media conglomerates. Some big companies such as Rupert Murdoch's News Corp still concentrate mainly on printed and digital news (*The Times, The Sun, The New York Post, The Wall Street Journal, The Australian*), publishing (HarperCollins), and broadcasting (Fox News). But most of the conglomerates incorporate a variety of activities from traditional news media (newspapers, magazines, television, and radio stations), books, films, music, streaming services, and other internet content, to (tele)communications hardware (the actual internet cable networks) and software. Among the biggest ones in the USA are Comcast, the Walt Disney Company, ViacomCBS, and AT&T[2]; internationally you can't miss Sony (Japan), Bertelsmann (Germany), Vivendi (France), Liberty Global (UK), Televisa (Mexico), Grupo Globo (Brazil). But also the high tech giants play a role, such as Alphabet (the owner of Google, which itself controls the video-sharing platform YouTube), Amazon (which not only dominates the Western book market, but has branched out to audiovisual media, and its founder now also owns *The Washington Post*), Alibaba (the Chinese online retailer which not only expanded to online entertainment services, but which also owns the *South China Morning Post*), or Baidu (China's counterpart to Google). Even Microsoft leads you directly to what its algorithms say is relevant news for you when you open its search engine Bing or use Microsoft Edge. Sometimes, it is not so easy to "locate" media, as the landscape is far from stable. CNN started as an independent company, was then incorporated into the Time Warner Group, which now belongs to AT&T. And these are only some of the high-profile players.

Within these structures, individual products no doubt try to maintain a certain degree of independence, but the bottom line is always the same: A market logic (sometimes "corrected" by overt or covert political influences) aimed at maximizing profits and growth. The effects are visible. Costs must be cut where possible. The range of cost-reducing possibilities is defined by the ease with which information can be accessed without spending money: "opinion journalism is cheap; fact-based investigative journalism is expensive and time-consuming" (Voltmer 2013, p. 226). Note, in passing, that there is conceptual continuity between the ubiquity of opinion journalism and the dominance of the politics of opinion which I pointed at earlier. But why would a newspaper or television station want to maintain a team of international correspondents if so much information can be obtained through the big news agencies with offices in most countries, such as Reuters (since 2008 the media division of Thomson Reuters – which also provides much of the bibliographical data for university rankings and academic evaluations), Associated Press (AP), Agence France-Presse (AFP), Agencia EFE, not to forget Russia's TASS and China's Xinhua (though attention for what the latter have on offer will be mostly restricted to what Western media interpret as manipulated false news).

At first sight, this seems quite rational and reasonable. But the power and omnipresence of these agencies do not necessarily turn them into "objective" sources. The main result is a perilous information paradox. Never have there been more tools for communication than today. Never has the spread of information been easier. But channels seem to be narrowing, inevitably funneling content. The counterargument that today everyone can gather and transmit eyewitness news with one's smartphone poised, only complicates the issue. This is a real advantage only if adequate control mechanisms – hence, enough people – are in place to properly verify and contextualize information gathered by "the people formerly known as the audience." A wide and diverse range of well-trained journalists, trying their best to separate facts from fiction and to provide analysis and interpretation, is not needed less, but more.

You may be tempted to assume that competition, as one of the essential ingredients of a market logic, can protect us against the excrescences of debilitating cost efficiency in the field of news, where narrowing means greater uniformity while competition could be expected to lead to different offerings to choose from. Clearly, striking differences in stance persist, that is why CNN and Fox News have different audiences. But what about the funneled content? At a time when the narrowing of channels had not yet reached its current level, in 1996, Pierre Bourdieu explained how, in the media, competition itself induces homogenization rather than diversification (cf. Bourdieu 2008 for the transcript of lectures he presented on French television in May 1996). The reasoning is as simple as it is accurate. Publication and broadcasting channels not only make use of very similar sources of input (first of all the wire services, and increasingly – as Bourdieu could not yet surmise – Facebook, Twitter, and Instagram), but they constantly watch each other. Probably journalists and their employers are the most avid consumers of journalism products. They cannot afford to miss anything "worthwhile" spotted by the others, because then they would lose the competition game. This is what Bourdieu called *the circular circulation of information.*

The circular circulation of media content worsens with the speed with which communication technologies allow us to operate. Acceleration in this field is a further aspect of what Rosa (2013) aptly described as alienation. Speed is anathema to thought and careful consideration. Media are under constant pressure. Whatever news there is to be brought, it's always urgent. The obviously felt need for "fact checking," which the fastest of the unedited media (such as Facebook and Twitter) only grudgingly admit and sparingly act upon, signals a problem that cannot be solved without wholesale international communication monitoring.[3]

In some countries, Facebook started to promote trustworthy news. Their method, however, is reminiscent of the university rating system. Facebook users are asked how trustworthy they think newspapers and news channels are. Depending on the answers, media outlets get a score. In other words, what users believe is the basis for detecting fake news. As a result, Fox News may score better than CNN in the United States, and Breitbart becomes a reliable source. *Truth by popular vote.* Google also has so-called fact check tools, allowing users to mark claims as false, or to search fact check results about a topic or a person. There are specialized fact-checking sites and browser plug-ins. Not surprisingly, advocating the use of such instruments is also under attack as a form of censorship. Meanwhile, former German journalist Claas Relotius (reporting, i.a., for *Der Spiegel*) managed to keep writing prize-winning stories hinging on countless fabrications. Ignorance and distortion abound in the global media (cf. Davies 2008). On the (much) brighter side, new business models in journalism, mostly digital publications with in-depth reporting, have been around for about a decade and may bring about change. Unfortunately, so far, they remain relatively marginal.

Sticking to the funnel metaphor would be a bit anachronistic if we did not realize that the new media, not only the social media but also the big internet search engines and the digital versions of older media, lead to new forms of fragmentation, the multiplication of subsidiary funnelets as it were.

Algorithms have the power to shape people's attention through the temporal and spatial localization and even personalization of information. It is an illusion to think that all information that is not behind firewalls is freely accessible. What the code knows about you, constructs your readily knowable environment. Individuals can of course escape from filter bubbles, to use Pariser's (2011) term, as their own agency clearly contributes to bubble building and maintenance (cf. Seargeant & Tagg 2019). Regaining informational autonomy from technologically guided attention, however, takes a serious amount of conscious effort. Even if you succeed, as an individual you mostly lack the tools to go beyond what is publicly on offer. Adding to this that ordinary people, like you and me, lack the time to regularly visit more than just a few sites, it is easy to end up in an invisibly secluded information space that feels so familiar that other spaces are automatically perceived as incomprehensible, if not hostile.

The disastrous effects of exclusive organization along the lines of cost efficiency in the health sector are so palpable that they may kindle some hope for change. In the media they do not surface in the same blatant or "critical" way. They may remain more subtle, barely visible. Exposing them may even look like serious exaggeration. You are right, it is not the case that literally everything has changed drastically.[4] But it is equally illusory to think that nothing has really changed. In particular, also in the media we find traces of the derailment of reflexivity, two of which I will touch upon in the following sections. Both are related to the media's market orientation.

Reflexivity on display

Media have always done their best to profile themselves. From the moment when media became commercial products, they had no choice. But the need to do so, and to do so more extensively than in the form of a simple slogan, seems to have increased with the awareness of vulnerability to the kinds of criticism formulated in the previous paragraphs. You will have seen that the criticism is not formulated as an accusation that the media would not be able or willing to bring the news as objectively as possible. Objectivity would be a strange demand anyway given the fundamental subjectivity that is inevitably involved at least at three levels: The level of reported "events," which involve individual experiences beyond what can be observed as intersubjectively verifiable facts; the level of the reporting, where journalists and editors would not even be doing their jobs properly if they would not try to interpret, a process requiring recourse to their own knowledge, training, and background; and the level of uptake, where the news consumer's comprehension, selectivity, and stance remain beyond anyone's control.[5] The problem I have tried to explain is a structural one. Every news outlet must compete with countless others. It must also generate revenue. The actual gathering of information, therefore, must be as cost-efficient as possible. This demand can be met thanks to the abundantly available sources that can be used as input. The highly homogenized output, however, can never be an interesting selling point. Therefore, most individual media, except for the most important ones which still have their own data-gathering networks, must succeed in setting themselves apart by different means.

The printed press that I have easy access to on a daily basis includes the Flemish quality newspaper *De Standaard*. Its display of reflexivity goes well beyond the expected advertising (which is by definition the meta-level of telling people "this is who we are and why you have to buy our paper").

One would expect any self-respecting newspaper (i) to have a system of internal quality control and, in addition or in combination, (ii) an open line of communication allowing readers to comment, with the expectation that their reactions could contribute to the evaluation of editorial practices. Questions about quality (point (i)) must include: Why do we cover event X but not event Y? Does our coverage meet standards of truth and journalistic ethics? Without aiming for the mere recording of "facts," is our presentation accurate, insightful, and fair? Without trying to avoid controversy (some would say, a certain degree of activism when important issues such as public health, education, discrimination, or inequality are concerned), do we manage to treat everyone with the respect they deserve? Do we include the relevant sources in our stories? Do our headlines capture the essence, or do they simply function as clickbait? Do we have the courage to hold publication back until we get all the details straight, or are we simply too eager to get the scoop? These are issues that should be in the back of every reporter's and every editor's mind all the time, and for which they are permanently accountable. Accountability also means (point (ii)) that readers have the right to expect their news providers to abide by the norms of journalistic professionalism and ethics. They may formulate complaints, which must be taken seriously to the extent that they can be weighed against the standards to be met.

Some news media have institutionalized combined attention for (i) and (ii) in a dedicated ombudsman position; when the focus is on (ii), the term may be "public editor" (mostly in North American terminology), or even "reader advocate" or "reader representative," in contrast to a "standards editor" responsible for (i). In principle, the ombudsman is independent, free to be openly critical of a newspaper's performance; s/he communicates directly with both staff and readers; it is not unusual for the results of deliberations to be published in a regular column. There is, of course, inherent ambiguity in the position. How far does the independence go? If the ombudsman is recruited from the staff, s/he cannot but take known sensitivities into account, as well as the fact that after an ombuds period, reintegration into the regular crew must be possible. If the ombudsman is an outsider, there may not be sufficient familiarity with regular working conditions and practices.

Historically, setting up this position usually constituted an attempt to handle a credibility crisis (cf. Nemeth 2003). In its earliest history, it was created in the form of a committee rather than an individual, specifically at the *New York World* in 1913 and at Japan's *Asahi Shimbun* in 1922 (cf. Reif 2004, p. 50). At the *New York World*, Ralph Pulitzer installed a Bureau for Accuracy and Fair Play to counter its being depicted as the archetype of sensation-seeking "yellow journalism." At the *Asahi Shimbun,* the ombuds function was also a line of defense. The paper had been trying to take the sharper edges off its liberal views, in response to the government's suppression of an article that was too critical. Many staff reporters did not accept this accommodation and resigned. Readers may also not have liked the change. The paper restored its lost credibility as best it could (leading to later clashes with the rapidly growing Japanese far right, and to inevitable accommodation again, turning the paper ultimately into one of the government's wartime propaganda tools).

Circumstances were incomparably different when the first modern-style public editor was appointed in North America for the *Louisville Courier-Journal* (and its afternoon counterpart the *Louisville Times*) in 1967, but media credibility was again a vivid issue at this time of turmoil, at the confluence of the Free Speech Movement, the Civil Rights Movement, and the Anti-Vietnam War Movement. Specifically, reporting on the Vietnam war, still strongly biased towards the hegemonic frame embodied by government sources, was under attack amidst incessant protests. At the same time, there was a desire for innovation and originality. The *Louisville Courier* was regarded as one of America's top journals which did not hesitate to experiment. What seems obvious now, but what was new at the time, was their introduction of signed editorials. Appointing an ombudsman was another innovation, inspired by what was beginning to happen in corporate and institutional America all over in the 1960s, and felt to be well-advised for the media under the circumstances.

The example was followed by many others. Unlike the *Washington Post*, which followed suit in 1970, the *New York Times* did not appoint a public editor until 2003, when it experienced its own "Relotius moment" with the discovery of fabrications and plagiarism in articles by NYT reporter Jayson Blair. The *New York Times* had no choice but to do something visible to restore faith in its valued trustworthiness. But the world of publishing was changing drastically around the same time, and the public editor position was dropped by the *Louisville Courier* in 2008, by the *Washington Post* in 2013, and by the *New York Times* in 2017, just 14 years after they had forcibly installed one. In fact, very few are left. Cuts in budgets are sometimes adduced as arguments for this change, but it is mainly motivated by the fact that readers now have more than enough tools to respond to news and the way in which it is reported – and they know how to make use of them. Furthermore, the argument goes, accountability lies with each reporter and editor. Though part (ii) of the ombuds function is losing relevance, part (i) is of course as important as ever. The better papers keep paying attention, and though there may be no more ombudsman or public editor, the "standards editor," responsible for internal quality control, is still there, and new ones keep getting appointed.

De Standaard is the only Belgian newspaper with an ombudsman. They decided to install one (after earlier experiments, apparently) in 2011, at a time when the function was already being eliminated by most newspaper publishers elsewhere. Was there a compelling reason to do so? There was no crisis situation comparable to those experienced by *Asahi Shimbun* in 1922 or *The New York Times* in 2003. There was also no way in which this slowly vanishing role could be presented as original, unlike when the initiative was taken by the *Louisville Courier-Journal* in 1967. Maybe there was a general distrust of the media which could be countered by more transparency. More importantly, however, there was a general sense of urgency for newspapers to re-establish their own position in a rapidly changing media landscape. What territory can newspapers claim? Can they convince readers that the quality of the news they bring is the best that can be offered by regularly explaining how certain editorial decisions were made, or by telling the story behind an occasional mistake?

No doubt quality control is a necessary form of reflexivity. And transparency is no doubt needed. But does reflexivity perhaps derail – even if rather harmlessly – when it is ostentatiously put on display? News ombudsmen have always downplayed the public relations side of their job. Educating readers about the news organization, however, not only serves the readers, but may be in the first place intended to restore or maintain trust, reader satisfaction, and subscription rates. There is a reason why *De Standaard* felt obliged to explain to its audience why an ombudsman was needed. The explanation, predictably, did not touch upon the public relations side – a textbook example of the hidden persuasiveness of advertising. The two ombudsmen in the period since 2011 did a reasonable job, but weighing the ingredients of justification and critique, justification obviously won, reserving critique for less critical issues. After two years, the first ombudsman took stock in an article arguing, not surprisingly, that the quality of newspaper journalism today (with his own paper as example) is the best one can expect, given a paper's broad and complex responsibility within rather narrow constraints. On a different occasion, he co-authored an article with the paper's editor-in-chief, reporting on the research they had done into the correctness of reporting in *De Standaard*. Predictably, small errors are admitted, but the overall assessment is highly favorable, and they promise to do even better in the future.

None of this would be so important if what I have just described would be an isolated phenomenon. Unfortunately, the way in which *De Standaard*'s ombuds position is profiled as quality-oriented (which I am sure it is to a significant extent) without recognizing an additional set of motives, is entirely in line with at least two other meta-level activities showing disoriented (if not derailed) reflexivity. One is the way in which the journal flags a feature which it calls *De correspondenten* ("the correspondents"). The idea is that a number of journalists are given ample time to dig into an important and broadly defined issue such as the disruptive economy, the problem of stress at work, the "epidemic" of insomnia, Germany's influence in the European Union, political bias in academia, migration crises, and many more. An excellent initiative you will agree. But is this not the normal task of news reporting? Why does the paper feel the need to present this as an extra? Do they admit implicitly that reporting is generally substandard due to a lack of personnel and the speed with which information is adopted from other sources? Are they right to believe that this kind of advertising will attract readers? And if they are, what does this tell us about the low expectations of readers these days, or their socialization into the framing of the meta-world?

A second example is a 54-page magazine-like "journalistic annual report" published for the first time at the end of 2019, and announced as a future tradition. It is showcased as evidence of transparency and reflexivity: The paper analyses itself; it opens its kitchen doors and shows how things work. About 20 high-ranking journalists/editors talk about the choices they had to make, admitting mistakes here and there, but emphasizing, as one would expect, the great care with which they are engaged in bringing the readers interesting, important, and reliable news. In fact, they are all collectively engaged in the work of the ombudswoman, who also contributes a piece, taking stock of her first year on the job.

For me as an academic, this layer cake of ostentatiously displayed reflexivity is completely reminiscent of the meta-level work that consumes so much of the energy of universities. It covers up the effects of information funneling which should be the main worry of news reporting in the service of a democratic society. Still, I read *De Standaard* every day, as it is one of the better options locally available. I plead guilty to the charge of complicity.

Info on demand

You are right if you believe there are positive tendencies which I have failed to emphasize so far. Not everything in the mass media is hopeless.

With some effort and a soundly critical approach, a lot of very detailed and well-contextualized information can be obtained directly from the internet. Moreover, increasing professionalization of reporters in the mainstream media ensures – sometimes even better than in the past – that they do a lot of the searching for you, know how to combine such information with what they pick up from the wire services and what becomes accessible through their networks. Also, investigative reporting is far from dead. As a result, the quality of what reaches readers and viewers is generally good, sometimes outstanding. The better media still refuse to simply go along with public sentiment. This is probably the reason why they also attract so much hostility. Trump is not the only one to accuse the media of bringing "fake news" if they do not tell his truth. Journalists do not have to seek war zones to run the risk of verbal and physical abuse. There is a reason why the Dutch broadcasting service NOS decided to remove its logo from its satellite vans.

What prevents most reporting from getting a triple-A rating (from a content rather than a market perspective), however, is not a lack of professionalism or passion. Nor is it only the circular circulation of information to which, following Bourdieu, I have already drawn your attention. Just like politics and academia, the media have massively given in to the demands of life at a meta-level. The primordial journalistic question seems to have become: What do readers and viewers want to read and see? From a market perspective, you will agree, this is a good question to ask. But only from a market perspective. Again, we are confronted with a perversion of a basic characteristic of all communication. In technical terms it is called audience design. Messages must be formulated in a way that connects as seamlessly as possible with the mental world of the addressee. Healthy empathy and necessary reflexivity, this is. But once the balance tips entirely in the direction of (imagined) audience demands, we see derailment again. Rather than to concentrate on content, features and programs get over-adapted to what the editors and programmers think their audiences want, in the hope to boost sales, viewing figures, or simply clicks.

Basic ingredients of the corresponding media ideology are the scoop, the personalization of stories, and simply "being there." Ever-accelerating flows of communication make it hard for any media outlet to be the "first" with any piece of news – at least, in the fields the audience's guided gaze can reasonably be expected to find "newsworthy." Still, getting the scoop functions as a kind of holy grail, and carefully checking and double-checking is easily sacrificed. The consequences are serious. A scoop requires a catchy title or image, and that is what will be remembered even if it turns out later that it does not really do justice to the facts.

Since it is hard to get real scoops, stories must distinguish themselves in different ways. Personalization is one of the techniques. Adding quotes and names (even if generally unknown to the public) livens up the narrative. Turning a serious issue into a human-interest story is even better. It is not surprising, therefore, that there is a temptation to invent palatable details which occasionally lead to media scandals followed by admissions of guilt and promises of more restraint and control. As in academia, it is surprising that fraud does not occur more regularly.

"Being there" is showcased as a mark of quality. Yet, foreign correspondents and news bureaus with the time and means for long-term familiarization with foreign contexts are slowly becoming museum pieces. Press pools no doubt keep delivering useful and insightful services. But their contribution is overshadowed by ad hoc on-the-scene appearances of parachute journalists, creating a semblance of real presence. Let something disastrous happen, from an earthquake to a spectacular bus crash, and local television stations will send a reporter or find a "witness" nearby for on-the-spot rephrasing of information that is already known. In terms of content, there is no justification for this use of the budget, but the market value of possible personalization prevails. The reporter or witness, who does not have access to more facts than what can be accessed through available and powerful communication tools, gets to answer questions about feelings of shock, desperation, outrage, depending on the event, the answers to which can easily be imagined by anyone with a morsel of empathy.

Less explicit, but clearly embedded in the media ideology and with significant consequences for media content, is the focus on what is of local interest and on a narrow range of high-profile political issues. Clearly, parachute reporters are not sent in at random; this is done after judging a local audience's real or imagined interest. Calamities with an immediate impact facilitate the choices. A good example was the spread of COVID-19 in early 2020. For months, it almost stopped all other reporting, until it got briefly intertwined with mass protests following the death of George Floyd in an event of racist police brutality. Similarly, news in early 2021 was dominated by COVID-19 vaccination problems, only to be interrupted by sensational events such as an Oprah Winfrey show figuring British royals. Does that mean nothing else was happening in the world? Judging from the only narrowly differentiated flows of meager but endlessly elastic information, it is hard to imagine that suddenly all assets of entire media powerhouses had to be mobilized around such exclusive targets, no matter how important they were. The strategy was clear. People are worried. Let us milk the subject. So, let us play around with predictions (about events and measures to be taken), spend ample time on the reporting of events and measures (even if this means livestreaming non-events – the content of which could be summarized much more clearly in a few minutes), and organize endless articles and talk shows to ventilate (preferably combative) opinions about what everyone already knows. The opposite and equally objectionable strategy would have been to downplay the health issues. But the reporting would have been much stronger if less thinly stretched.

This does not mean that choices are easy. There is a reason why in the mid-20th century, American English acquired the term "Afghanistanism," describing a journalistic practice of "concentrating on problems in distant parts of the world while ignoring controversial local issues" (Merriam-Webster). Since its inception, events in Afghanistan have subverted the rationale for the term, further illustrating how the media work: Afghanistan achieved "real" news value in the West when occupied by the enemy (the Soviet Union, from 1979 to 1989, the last decade of the Cold War), when harboring that other nascent enemy, Al Qaeda (towards the end of the 20th century), and ever since the start of Operation Enduring Freedom in October 2001, leading to the longest war in US history. Unless there will be drastic changes in the way in which the media work, you can predict that after complete withdrawal from Afghanistan, if it happens, attention will soon diminish and "Afghanistanism" may re-assume its earlier position. In the same way, and unfortunately, it will not be surprising if attention for changes possibly to be brought about by the Black Lives Matter movement will not be tenaciously followed up, no matter how loudly some media trumpeted in May 2020 that something truly revolutionary could be happening.

There is a deeply symbiotic relationship between media and politics – and you are free to add academic research in the mix.[6] All parties have their media specialist, and academics are getting media training. Journalists are often dependent on political sources, just as politicians need the media for communicating with a potential electorate. The content of reporting is often the result of research, while research itself is regularly custom-made in collaboration with politically controlled public institutions or journals and broadcasting companies. While this looks like harmonious cohabitation, there are constant attempts, mostly from the corners of the wood in which power is wielded, to direct the public gaze.

Reporting, research, and the reporting of research may also trigger political attention. Sometimes this is useful. At other times it is a simple reflection of meta-political preoccupations. Nowhere is this meta-level of the symbiosis more in evidence than in the ritualized practice of leaking. Politicians (some more than others) routinely try to boost their own or to undermine someone else's position by leaking information, usually half-baked, not ready for public consumption. The media, in turn, make a meal of it, hoping to strengthen their market share. Part of the game, miles removed from fundamental concerns with the common interest, is a principle of mutual exclusivity and favoritism, as well as the wholesale condemnation of leaks one does not benefit from (on the political side) or that are too quickly presented as true (on the media side).

All of this guided attention is embedded in a world of mass distraction, with features and programs outbidding each other (amidst a fortunately ineradicable dose of good humor and fine art and music) with attempts to appeal to people's lower instincts: Senseless ridicule, one-upmanship, the urge to sensationalism. The corresponding coarseness spreads, not in the least to the world of politics. And so does a harmful degree of ignorance, with the complicity of the media.

Making such remarks invites a reproach of elitism. Who do you think you are? Do you think you are so much smarter? Is this not the kind of scoffing that makes a majority vote the way they do? Is what others think not as important as what you think you know? These kinds of questions have left too many of us complicitly silenced. When it comes to information and truth, there is complicity in apologies for falsities, in empathy for those led to believe them, in alignment with its sources. *Truth can never be established by popular vote.* That is why it is not unreasonable to make almost impossible demands of the guardians of information.

Asocial media

It has been noted that "the marketization of news journalism has changed the circulation of information by promoting a 'culture of virality' and by increasingly fragmenting media audiences" (Graber 2015, p. 354). The number of views and clicks determines advertising income. Sharing through social media must be facilitated to lead members of viral communities back to the source for more views and clicks. At dazzling speed, snippets of media discourse get re-combined, re-entextualized, and re-contextualized. Not only the audiences are fragmented. So too are the messages.

Today, about 49% of the world population uses some form of social media.[7] In February 2020, social media was used as a source of news by 25% of adults in Japan, 35% in Germany, 39% in the United Kingdom, 41% in Belgium, 48% in the United States, 70% in Mexico, all the way to 77% in Kenya. Though social media companies have serious trouble ensuring the factuality of content, and though they are divided (also internally) about the need to do so, internet users' trust during times of crisis reaches an astonishing average of 49% (from a low 28% in the United Kingdom to 35% in the United States, 36% in Japan, 37% in Germany, 39% in Belgium, 57% in Mexico, all the way to 64% in China and even 84% in Russia). Only part of the news that circulates on social media comes from professional news sources. Since even those rely on narrow channels and have trouble checking anything off the beaten path, the density of global news pollution must rival the quality of the air above Delhi or Beijing on a windless, hot, and crowded day. With enough smog around, QAnon and other conspiracy theory factories thrive.

Partly, fragmentation also results from the curiously self-centered nature of social media. The affordances of the technology include the possibility of genuine interaction and debate, an abundance of which is to be found. But the starting point is almost invariably individuals or small groups putting themselves, their achievements and ideas, or fragments of their worlds, whether directly experienced or mediated, on display. Most of this is trivial and completely innocent (disregarding the potential loss of 144 minutes per day for the average social media user). Some of it also has become a useful and integral part of productive professional life. For some users, however, the absence of direct social control turns social media into welcome fora for unrestrained asocial or even anti-social behavior.

Social media may divide more than they bring together. Under the guise of freedom of speech, insults, racism, sexism, and hate speech spread widely across the internet. No doubt, the increasing coarseness in semi-public speech, carefully monitored by data-gathering companies in the service of political formations, is one of the catalysts for similar properties in the discourses of political populism. Remember the scandal surrounding the unauthorized harvesting of Facebook data by Cambridge Analytica (disclosed in early 2018), gathering information for psychological profiling in the service of election campaigns, enabling the micro-targeting of specific groups of voters. Even without sophisticated and intrusive techniques, there is enough useful language data to be scraped from the internet for politicians to know how to address the type of electorate they think will make them win.

Quoting Castells (2009, p. 417), "Power is primarily exercised by the construction of meaning in the human mind through processes enacted in global/local multimedia networks of mass communication, including mass self-communication." Since meaning is inevitably constructed collaboratively, all actors involved are somehow accomplices, whether or not they are in a dominant position, with or without apparent power to change things. Castells continues:

> Although theories of power and historical observation point to the decisive importance of the state's monopoly of violence as a source of social power, I argue that the ability to successfully engage in violence or intimidation requires the framing of individual and collective minds.
>
> (Castells 2009, p. 417)

By way of illustration, Castells refers – as I also did earlier in this essay – to the frame of the "war on terror" (not to forget the "axis of evil") which had to penetrate the American mind before the Bush administration could invade (or "liberate") Iraq. This may be an extreme case. But everyday forms of violence are equally rooted in the fertile soil for offensive discourse (with hate speech as its purest expression), provided by the internet and eagerly spread beyond by self-serving public figures.[8]

Notes

1 Not only the BBC needs its commercial activities (through BBC Studios); even the Chinese state broadcaster CCTV runs pay-TV channels in addition to its public service channels.

2 For a well-informed discussion of what he calls the growing "media monopoly," see Bagdikian (2000).

3 Monitoring is not only needed to check facts (which is routinely done in the context of organizations concerned with peace and stability, such as the International Crisis Group [www.crisisgroup.org/], organizations promoting debate and discussion, such as The Sydney Institute and its Media Watch Dog [https://thesydneyinstitute.com.au/about-the-sydney-institute/], dedicated media critique organizations such as Fairness & Accuracy in Reporting [FAIR, https://fair.org/], as well as by researchers at Human Rights Watch and Amnesty International). It could also serve the purpose of carefully comparing the ideological lenses through which the same events are looked at in different parts of the world and the inevitably colored wordings in which they are reported. A proposal to this effect, not put into practice, was made many years ago in Verschueren, Östman & Meeuwis (eds.) (2002).

4 Clearly, what we witness today is the result of a relatively unbroken line of development that could already be described decades ago in the relationship between media and modern societies (see, e.g., Thompson 1995).

5 This is not the place to add to the long literature on objectivity-related issues. A few references, pre-dating developments that we want to concentrate on here, may be useful: Gitlin (1980), Lippmann & Merz (1920), Schiller (1981), Schudson (1978), Wicker (1975).

6 Book-length treatises have been written about the power of the media-politics nexus (Castells 2009, Couldry 2012, Couldry & Hepp 2017), but an explicit link with academia is usually missing.

7 This is the figure which Statista gives on 18 May 2020 (www.statista.com/top ics/1164/social-networks/). All other figures in this paragraph also have Statista as their source.

8 To read up on the relationship between language and violence, a good starting point is Silva (ed.) (2017).

Recap
Sharing responsibility

Imagine you are a simple politician, voter, academic, administrator, journalist, social media user. You are aware of the problems besetting liberal democracy, academia, and the media. But you feel you are a cog in the machine, unable to make changes. Often, the most "responsible" form of behavior may then seem to stay in the mainstream. You try to make positive contributions by sailing ahead without making waves. You acquire the respectability that positions you in such a way that you feel you can "do" something. You are likely not just to move forward, but to move up, to be praised for your positive engagement, whether or not it is largely strategic. The problem is: This is the fastest way to complicity.

If this is so, how could I claim that this essay embraces hope? How can recognizing complicity help you to rise out of helpless resignation to machinations beyond your control so that you can take your individual share of responsibility and act or react? Perhaps it is important to repeat what our primordial common goal should be: Reducing, ideally eliminating, any type of imbalance and injustice – whether intentionally inflicted or not – that diminishes vast numbers of people's chances to lead a life in dignity and equality. A good dose of subversive, "irresponsible" behavior may be the best way to contribute to such a lofty goal. With this in mind, we are all confronted with personal dilemmas when making choices. A cog-in-the-machine account does not count.

Dilemmas arise from everyone's connectedness with everyone else.

Being "responsible," as described above, primarily orients you to the general interests of the institution or organization you belong to. This may be an administrative body, an educational institution, a trade union, a political party, a small company, or a large corporation. They do not accept any member's refusal to pursue their specific "corporate" interests. This is what Marcuse (1964) described as a sophisticated system of domination which leaves little or no room for real freedom of action. This is also what Reich (1970), emphasizing the collusion between the power of government

DOI: 10.4324/9781003206354-4

and the private power of corporations, identified as the stifling grip of what he called the "Corporate State." Fifty years later, many of the processes Marcuse and Reich were concerned with are still in operation. A major difference may be that the balance between state power and corporate power is tipping more and more in favor of the corporations. Partly, this results from the neo-liberal abstinence from political interference with the spreading tentacles of the multinationals. But it also results from the (equally neo-liberal) tendency to "incorporate" whatever still appears as public.[1] That is why public universities can increasingly be described, as Eglin (2013) does with special reference to the Canadian context, as "corporate universities."

However, no one is only an administrator, a teacher, a trade unionist, a politician or activist, an employee, or an executive. As a human being, you cannot turn a blind eye towards other people's misery. Your solidarity must extend beyond your immediate political-economic realm. How "loyal" can you then remain to your government agency if you know that it ignored warnings that could have prevented a deadly gas leak; to your school or university if you see how it collaborates with companies responsible for massive environmental pollution; to your union if it happens to be a male bastion ignoring demands for gender equality; to your political party if you know how much it contributes to interethnic antagonism, if not racial discrimination; to your company if it was negligent in the construction or refurbishment of an apartment building that, as a result, caught fire and destroyed the lives of already underprivileged people; to your multinational corporation if you know that it keeps accumulating wealth by exploiting people, by producing harmful products, by massively invading people's privacy?

Reich's diagnosis, already 50 years ago, was that people's dilemmas lead to split personalities (Reich calls it schizophrenia, while there is also a tinge of hypocrisy involved): In private life they are open, warm, compassionate, and generous; as organizational or institutional beings they meekly do what is expected, disclaiming any responsibility for what their organization or institution (or even society as a whole) does or stands for.

There is such a thing as "corporate responsibility." Traffic safety is not just a matter of individuals following traffic rules and avoiding drunk driving. It is also a matter of engineering and manufacturing. Quite often companies or organizations are held responsible in court. Many also try to display social responsibility pro-actively. This may be genuinely beneficial. But sometimes reputation management has simply been integrated into the business model, positively motivated or negatively to avoid the possible damage of shaming.[2] This does not solve your dilemma. You cannot leave it to legal agencies or activist groups to do the responsibility work for you. Shaming and public inquiries assign blame. Usually this will leave you as an individual untouched. But what if you are one of the car factory's engineers or assembly-line workers, what if you are a car salesman selling a potentially dangerous vehicle, what if you are an administrator in the public office responsible for car safety regulations?

Sharing responsibility is the default mode. Ignoring this makes you complicit. Realizing your complicity is in everyone's interest, even your own. Consider the tendency of neoliberal governments to put their own commitment to legal pensions on the back burner, while promoting pension funds dependent on the stock market. Going along with this makes you dependent on capital, with the remote possibility of windfalls for yourself, but with the certainty of entanglement in the invisible wheeling and dealing of a multitude of market players responsible for quite visible injustice and inequality. If this is not a burden on your conscience, consider your self-interest: Maximizing profits in the stock market requires cutting costs, especially for labor; in the long run, you or your neighbor, depending on who is where in the pecking order, will experience stagnation in your income, if not serious loss.

Recognizing complicity puts an end to "us" versus "them." It is still important to see guilt and innocence. Debating these will remain crucial, and a certain degree of indignation may be a healthy driving force. But everyone is involved, and the dividing lines become fluid areas of shared responsibility. Gaps may be bridged, and polarization may become a marginal phenomenon looked at with suspicion. The public sphere may witness the rebirth of truly democratic debate, negotiation, and decision-making. Democracies may succeed in countering systematic disinformation.[3] They may turn health care and education, however expensive they are, into priorities again. They may manage to recombine care for people within their borders with solidarity on a global scale. They may show solidarity with future generations by doing what it takes to pass on a cleaner planet. They may develop a fair redistribution of wealth, or even open up to "utopian" ideas such as universal employment, and everyone's right to a basic income (cf. Bregman 2017 and Van Parijs & Vanderborght 2017). Before this happens, however, significant change is needed. In particular, *the power that we find in the recognition of complicity must be used to resist the manufacturing of consent*.[4] To that end, it is important to understand how ideas circulate, how this affects every aspect of how society works, and how ideological sanity can be reached to underscore much-needed action.

Notes

1 According to Naomi Klein (2007) such "incorporation" is greatly facilitated by disasters, since it can then be invoked as a remedy to cope with an emergency – but with lasting structural effects. For an account of US capitalism's handling of a catastrophe as it unfolds, see Wolff (2021), illustrating the strong grip (and

resulting failure) of an exclusively market-oriented, corporatist system in the face of a global health crisis.

2 Shaming is actually used frequently by activists or interest groups. See Jacquet (2015) for an illustrated description of how this works. While shaming starts from the assumption of guilt, its formalized counterpart, the public inquiry, leaves responsibility open at the start, but often leads to the construction of blame (see Murphy 2019) and scores the same effects.

3 Horton (2020) identifies systematic disinformation as one of the main reasons why the handling of COVID-19 turned out to be such a catastrophe.

4 Obviously, I am borrowing this phrase from Herman & Chomsky (1994). What they describe in relation to the role of the mass media, with particular reference to the way in which thought about events in the world is mediated by American news companies, is also in their view just part of a general propaganda model characterizing communication from government and companies alike.

Prospect
An ecology of the public sphere?

My excursion through society (with an emphasis on politics, tangentially including its legislative powers), the university, and the media is not merely a random reflection of the trajectory of my inevitably limited range of experience and observation. These points of attention were consciously chosen. Political control over the judiciary, education, and the media, are the only steps needed to turn a democracy into an authoritarian regime. Such steps, usually tiny, are incremental. We see them whenever politicians complain about naïve judges, prejudiced media, and leftist education.[1] We see them when judges, journalists, and professors, notwithstanding their loud protest, become extra careful to avoid providing ammunition for politically inspired accusations – engaging in the most dangerous of censorships, self-censoring. We see them whenever there is, as the argument goes, no alternative, and when, in Timothy Snyder's (2018) words, the "politics of inevitability" is being practiced. We see it happening whenever Republicans in the US fail to speak out against another Trumpism, when Putin manages to make himself irreversible for another 16 years or so, when Polish leaders fasten their grip on judges, when Hungary's Victor Orbán uses the fight against COVID-19 as a pretext for controlling protest and manages surreptitiously to silence the last independent news media, but also when Flemish (and many other European) politicians surf the waves of narrow-minded nationalism (even if parading as open-mindedness). We also see it when academics and journalists, universities, and media outlets, succumb to politically unleashed market forces, endangering their autonomy in the pursuit of their important mission to contribute to a healthy public sphere.

I view the public sphere as a communicative space, a *space of meaning*. Communicatively, interactively, intersubjectively generated meanings communicated in the context of shared media, networks, organizations, institutions, states, and state-like structures, form its substance. It is an arena with never-ending struggles over meaning. Such struggles for hegemony have social, economic, and political consequences, some of which I have tried

DOI: 10.4324/9781003206354-5

to illustrate. Because of these consequences, I do not hesitate to posit a need for "ecological" care or monitoring in the realm of publicly circulating meaning. There are two reasons for using this metaphor.

First, a reference to ecology emphasizes the *complexity of a global public sphere as a realm of meaning*. This complexity can be conceived as a dynamic and multidirectional continuum of meaning-making processes carried by a multiplicity of languages and communicative styles operating through a diversity of public media (printed, broadcast, internet-based) against the background of a wide range of networks (some political) and institutions (some educational). Keeping this in mind, we cannot avoid addressing what Thompson (1995) called the need for a "reinvention of publicness" in the context of a fast-changing economic, political, and media landscape that breaks through the structural boundaries of the organized modernity of nation states to become truly global (cf. Triandafyllidou, Wodak & Krzyżanowski 2009). These changes, in combination with the development of communication technologies, inevitably move the notion of publicness beyond the traditional requirement or expectation of locally confined co-presence.

Second, this kind of complex, communicatively constituted, dynamic public sphere lacks transparency and easily lends itself to manipulation in struggles over meaning that inadvertently (though not necessarily unintentionally) maintain patterns of dominance or establish new ones. The public information environment is profoundly polluted, not in the least by the participatory propaganda[2] of sharing and retweeting falsehoods and half-truths. Restoring transparency is a serious challenge because of what may be the core of present-day forms of globalization, namely "the weakening of meaning-providing contexts" (cf. Wagner 2012, p. 168), a direct consequence of blurred (or "liquid," cf. Bauman 2000) boundaries or frames of interpretation.

The suggestion that "ecological" monitoring of the public sphere is required presupposes that there is a potential problem comparable to the disequilibrium that human activity tends to create in natural ecosystems. This problem can be identified as the functioning of ideology in its capacity of "meaning in the service of power" (Thompson 1990, p. 7). Social relations in the sphere of publicness, or the public positionings of people in relation to each other (usually involving the level of perceived groups), are commonly characterized by relations of dominance which are established and sustained by ideologies underlying publicly accessible discourse and communication.

In this context, ideology does not refer to the great political schools of thought (the manifold "-isms") that can be identified as driving forces in modern history, but to patterns of meaning, frames of interpretation, or belief systems bearing on aspects of social reality that are felt to be commonsensical (i.e., that are unreflectively thought of as "normal"), that are thus carried along communicatively without being questioned, and that can guide action in surreptitious ways. Ideology-related communicative disequilibria that characterize current power dynamics must be monitored in societies that pride themselves on their democratic foundations.

Ideological processes are basically habits of thought. They can be shaped and influenced in socially and politically detrimental directions, leaving victims along the way. But the ecosystem of meaning-making is not an unchangeable and necessarily subconscious mechanism. In fact, reflexive awareness is at the basis of every form of communication and cooperation. But when it gets stuck in the grooves of habitual thought, life at a meta-level (politically, academically, in the media) may take over and risk derailing – however contradictory the metaphors of "getting stuck in the grooves" and "derailment" may be. When that happens, cooperation becomes complicity. Even the simplest form of interaction requires common ground that we cooperatively use as a foundation to build communication on, as all communication carries loads of implicitness. But if we tacitly accept premises that we know are wrong, and if we do not speak out against them, normal communicative cooperation indeed becomes complicity.

There is a cure with two ingredients: *Constant reflection on what we routinely accept as "normal,"* and *the courage to speak out* – two pillars on which activism (as analyzed and advocated by Harvey 2012) should be built. This is not an easy exercise, but it can be learnt – it should be the main target of education in a democratic society. As eloquently argued by Giroux (2018), education must be defended as a public good (free of "the dictates of a business culture") to combat the civic illiteracy produced by political theatrics and too easily supported by the media.

There is a sense in which we are condemned to complicity, simply because individually we cannot always make a difference. It is hard to avoid complicity in a world in which everything is strongly interconnected through globalized capital markets and networks that are greatly facilitated by the available means for rapid mobility and instant communication. Probably we should simply accept the second part of Kutz's complicity principle, quoted earlier: "I am accountable for the harm or wrong we do together, independent of the actual difference I make" (2000, p. 122). The central issue is not good will and intentionality. What counts is what we do in practice. And even if we cannot escape from complicity altogether, resistance and (why not?) civil disobedience can offer little steps in the right direction. Systematic inequality and injustice can only survive by thousands of individual decisions *not* to take such steps.

Complicity, too, comes in little steps. By way of example and looking at the broad picture I have tried to sketch, today we see three mental movements. Sometimes they involve different people, sometimes also the same, but clearly they are logically connected to each other. The first is the *apology* for not taking seriously the "common people" who step along with a diversity of trends in populist thought. Such apologies, which you can regularly hear in academia and in the media, may be genuine. There are indeed good reasons to assume that we, collectively, have not done enough to ensure a safe and stable future for less privileged people, so that they have massively turned from socialism to nationalism, even if these labels are not used (cf. Eribon 2009). Sometimes the apologies are merely ritual, while usually they are inspired by the fear of being accused of taking the moral high ground, disrespectful of others. The second step is not only *empathy* with, but also *approval* of, the voting behavior in favor of various brands of populist policies. The voter is always right. The third is *getting in line with* the points of view that lead to such voting behavior. This is the normalization of Trumpist coarseness and disrespect in the public sphere, the normalization of perennial inequality, the natural superiority of some.

This three-step descent into the abyss may look mechanical and deterministic. Yet, there is no law of nature at work. Just as cooperation under conditions of derailed reflexivity in a foggy meta-world amounts to complicity, it is equally possible to move back from complicity to take little steps in the direction of positive cooperation, solidarity, and constructive community building, locally, nationally, and internationally. Education and media have a key role to play. Their main stumbling block is political control, even in democratic societies. Education depends largely on public funding, hence on political decisions. Media can be manipulated even without direct intervention; just make sure, for instance, that majority shares end up in government-friendly hands. But under conditions of liberal democracy, there is enough space for maneuver. No need, therefore, to give up or abandon hope (cf. Solnit 2016, Chomsky 2017). There is also no reason to believe that education and media can be purified to become instruments of absolute "truth." No such thing exists. But education and media, together, can counter the culture of fear, as well as the culture of doubt and denial, turning the world into a safer and more pleasant place.

Let me end with a small, implementable suggestion. Educate people into reading all communication in the public sphere as if it would contain the warning "unreflective consumption of the messages contained herein is harmful to your health." The recommendation would be to question whatever is taken for granted. This could put healthy reflexivity on the rails again. The picture this reveals is not necessarily pleasant. We may soon realize that President Biden's COVID-19 vaccination program in 2021 (with its version of America First) is simply the "responsible" implementation of what Trump was irresponsibly preparing for in 2020. This means we must be involved in a never-ending critical exercise.

In a way, what I am suggesting is a revival of Reich's (1970) belief that a revolution is possible at the level of consciousness or thought. Reich thought such a revolution was about to take place. He could not foresee how fundamentally Reagan and Thatcher would interfere with his vision. But since their interference was also to be found at the level of ideas, there is no reason why we could not jump-start a new kind of revolt against its ideological and socio-political-economic consequences. Combine this with Marcuse's (1964) call for a "Great Refusal," effectively ending the alienation which Rosa (2013) described as a consequence of automatically "doing what one does not really want to do," and there may again be an interesting and rewarding future for your children and grandchildren. All it takes is awareness of your complicity, and an uncompromising commitment to taking your share of responsibility. This means there is not just an outside enemy to fight. Social divides can be bridged by taking note of what we all share, an enemy within. Change follows from constant self-reflection, which should be adopted as a daily challenge, the basis for action. In a democratic society, no matter how imperfect it may be, no one can prevent us from taking this responsibility. That should give you hope and power.

No matter how important ideas may be, they can only produce desired outcomes if they form the basis for action, preferably collective. A sequel to this book, therefore, should reflect on activism, an update perhaps of Alinsky's *Rules for Radicals*. I may not have the knowledge and experience to write such a book. You will have noticed that there is a lot about practices in this text, but still it is primarily focused on discourse and the discursive grounding of practices. Perhaps your expertise lends itself better to a more practical follow-up. If so, I volunteer to be your first reader.

Notes

1 In recent years, this has been the triple complaint of, amongst others, British Prime Minister Boris Johnson and his chief adviser Dominic Cummings. And it spreads like an uncontained virus.
2 I adopt this phrasing from Jan Zienkowski's lecture "Propaganda and/or ideology in critical discourse studies," presented at the *Discourse Net 24* conference, September 2020.

References

Adachi, Satoshi. 2011. "Social integration in post-multiculturalism: An analysis of social integration policy in post-war Britain." *International Journal of Japanese Sociology* 20: 107–120.

Adut, Ari. 2018. *Reign of Appearances: The Misery and Splendor of the Public Sphere*. Cambridge: Cambridge University Press.

Alinsky, Saul D. 1971. *Rules for Radicals: A Pragmatic Primer for Realistic Radicals*. New York: Vintage Books.

Anderson, Benedict. 1983. *Imagined Communities: Reflections on the Origin and Spread of Nationalism*. London: Verso.

Angell, Marcia. 2005. "The truth about the drug companies." *Jurimetrics* 45(4): 465–471.

Angell, Marcia. 2009. "Drug companies & doctors: A story of corruption." *The New York Review of Books*, 15 January 2009.

Armstrong, John A. 1982. *Nations before Nationalism*. Chapel Hill, NC: University of North Carolina Press.

Badiou, Alain. 1998. *Abrégé de métapolitique*. Paris: Éditions du Seuil. (English translation, 2005, *Metapolitics*, London: Verso.)

Badiou, Alain. 2016. *Our Wound Is not so Recent*. Cambridge: Polity Press.

Bagdikian, Ben H. 2000 [1983]. *The Media Monopoly*. Boston, MA: Beacon Press.

Baldwin, James. 1963. *The Fire Next Time*. London: Penguin Books.

Bauman, Richard. 2013. "Horizons of context: From the interaction order to the nation-state." Plenary lecture presented at the *13th International Pragmatics Conference*, New Delhi, India, 8–13 September 2013.

Bauman, Zygmunt. 1989. *Modernity and the Holocaust*. Cambridge: Polity Press.

Bauman, Zygmunt. 2000. *Liquid Modernity*. Cambridge: Polity Press.

Benbassa, Esther. 2012. *De l'impossibilité de devenir français: Nps Nouvelles mythologies nationales*. Paris: Les Liens Qui Libèrent.

Bendix, Reinhard. 1974 [1956]. *Work and Authority in Industry: Ideologies of Management in the Course of Industrialization*. Berkeley, CA: University of California Press.

Besson, Éric. 2009. *Pour la nation*. Paris: Bernard Grasset.

Beyen, Marnix. 2010. "Identiteit regeert de Europese politiek" [Identity rules European politics]. *De Morgen*, 5 October 2010, p. 22.

Beynon, Huw. 1984 [1973]. *Working for Ford: Men, Masculinity, Mass Production and Militancy*. London: Allen Lane.

Blommaert, Jan & Jef Verschueren. 1992. *Het Belgische migrantendebat: De pragmatiek van de abnormalisering*. Antwerp: International Pragmatics Association.

Blommaert, Jan & Jef Verschueren. 1998. *Debating Diversity: The Discourse of Tolerance*. London: Routledge.

Bloom, Allan. 1987. *The Closing of the American Mind*. New York: Simon & Schuster.

Bourdieu, Pierre. 2008. *Sur la television*. Paris: Éditions Raisons d'Agir.

Bousquet, Marc. 2008. *How the University Works: Higher Education and the Low-Wage Nation*. New York: New York University Press.

Bregman, Rutger. 2017. *Utopia for Realists, and How We Can Get There*. London: Bloomsbury.

Briant, Emma. 2021. *Propaganda Machine: Inside Cambridge Analytica and the Digital Influence Industry*. London: Bloomsbury.

Camus, Renaud. 2011. *Le grand remplacement*. Neuilly-sur-Seine: David Reinharc.

Carens, Joseph H. 2010. *Immigrants and the Right to Stay*. Cambridge, MA: The MIT Press.

Castells, Manuel. 2009. *Communication Power*. Oxford: Oxford University Press.

Chakrabarti, Shami. 2014. *On Liberty*. London: Allen Lane.

Chamayou, Grégoire. 2009. "Petits conseils aux enseignants-chercheurs qui voudront réussir leur évaluation." *Contretemps*. http://www.contretemps.eu/print/323

Chomsky, Noam. 2017. *Optimism over Despair*. London: Penguin Books.

Choudry, Aziz & Dip Kapoor (eds.). 2013. *NGOization: Complicity, Contradictions and Prospects*. London: Zed Books.

Collini, Stefan. 2012. *What Are Universities For?* London: Penguin Books.

Couldry, Nick. 2012. *Media, Society, World: Social Theory and Digital Media Practice*. Cambridge: Polity Press.

Couldry, Nick & Andreas Hepp. 2017. *The Mediated Construction of Reality*. Cambridge: Polity Press.

Davies, Nick. 2008. *Flat Earth News*. London: Chatto & Windus.

Davis, Angela. 2012. *The Meaning of Freedom*. San Francisco CA: City Lights.

De Cleen, Benjamin, Benjamin Moffitt, Panos Panayotu & Yannis Stavrakakis. 2019. "The potentials and difficulties of transnational populism: The case of the Democracy in Europe Movement 2025 (DiEM 25)." *Political Studies* 68(1): 146–166.

De Dijn, Herman, Yvan Bruynseraede, Dirk Van Dyck, Irina Veretennicoff, Frank Willaert, Dominique Willems & Jacques Willems. 2016. *Het professoraat anno 2016: Reflectie over een beroep in volle verandering*. Brussel: KVAB.

De Wever, Bart. 2019. *Over identiteit*. Gent: Borgerhoff & Lamberigts.

Demiati, Nasser. 2009. *Éduquer ou civiliser la banlieue?* Paris: Téraèdre.

DiAngelo, Robin. 2018. *White Fragility: Why It's So Hard for White People to Talk about Racism*. New York: Penguin Random House.

Donoghue, Frank. 2008. *The Last Professors: The Corporate University and the Fate of the Humanities*. New York: Fordham University Press.

DORA. 2012. *San Francisco Declaration on Research Assessment*. https://sfdora.org/ (last consulted 27 April 2020).

Eddo-Lodge, Reni. 2018. *Why I'm No Longer Talking to White People about Race*. London: Bloomsbury.

Eglin, Peter. 2013. *Intellectual Citizenship and the Problem of Incarnation*. Lanham, MD: University Press of America.

Eisenstadt, Shmuel N. (ed.). 2002. *Multiple Modernities*. New Brunswick, NJ: Transaction Publishers (originally a special issue of Daedalus, Winter 2000).

Ekberg, Lena & Jan-Ola Östman. 2020. "Identity construction and dialect acquisition among immigrants in rural areas: The case of Swedish-language Finland." *Journal of Multilingual and Multicultural Development*. https://doi.org/10-1080/01434632.2020.1722681

Eribon, Didier. 2009. *Retour à Reims*. Paris: Fayard.

ESMU. 2010. *A University Benchmarking Handbook: Benchmarking in European Higher Education*. Brussels: European Centre for Strategic Management of Universities.

Fellner, Jamie. 2009. "Race, drugs, and law enforcement in the United States." *Stanford Law and Policy Review* 20(2): 257–291.

Ferlie, Ewan, Lynn Ashburner, Louise Fitzgerald & Andrew Pettigrew. 1996. *The New Public Management in Action*. Oxford: Oxford University Press.

Fillmore, Lily Wong. 1991. "When learning a second language means losing the first." *Early Childhood Research Quarterly* 6: 323–346.

Gándara, Patricia & Megan Hopkins (eds.). 2010. *Forbidden Language: English Learners and Restrictive Language Policies*. New York: Teachers College Press.

Gellner, Ernest. 1997. *Nationalism*. New York: New York University Press.

Giles, Jim. 2005. "The nightmare before funding." *Nature* 437: 308–311.

Gill, Rosalind. 2016. "Breaking the silence: The hidden injuries of neo-liberal academia." *Feministische Studien* 34(1): 39–55.

Giroux, Henry A. 2018. *The Public in Peril: Trump and the Menace of American Authoritarianism*. New York: Routledge.

Gitlin, Todd. 1980. *The Whole World is Watching: Mass Media in the Making & Unmaking of the New Left*. Berkeley, CA: University of California Press.

Golsan, Richard J. 2006. *French Writers and the Politics of Complicity: Crises of Democracy in the 1940s and 1990s*. Baltimore, MD: The Johns Hopkins University Press.

Graber, Kathryn E. 2015. "On the disassembly line: Linguistic anthropology in 2014." *American Anthropologist* 117(2): 350–363.

Graeber, David. 2013. *The Democracy Project: A History, a Crisis, a Movement*. London: Allen Lane.

Gumperz, John. 1982. *Discourse Strategies*. Cambridge: Cambridge University Press.

Hart, H.L.A. 1994 [1961]. *The Concept of Law* (second edition). Oxford: Oxford University Press.

Harvey, David. 2012. *Rebel Cities: From the Right to the City to the Urban Revolution*. London: Verso.

Hazelkorn, Ellen. 2015. *Rankings and the Reshaping of Higher Education: The Battle for World-Class Excellence*. London: Palgrave Macmillan.

Head, Simon. 2011. "The grim threat to British universities." *The New York Review of Books*, 13 January 2011.

Heller, Monica & Bonnie McElhinny. 2017. *Language, Capitalism, Colonialism: Toward a Critical History*. Toronto, ON: University of Toronto Press.

Héran, François. 2018. *Migrations et sociétés* (Leçon inaugurale du Collège de France). Paris: Fayard.

Herman, Edward S. & Noam Chomsky. 1994. *Manufacturing Consent: The Political Economy of the Mass Media*. New York: Vintage.

Herrnstein, Richard & Charles Murray. 1994. *The Bell Curve: Intelligence and Class Structure in American Life*. New York: Free Press.

Hobsbawm, Eric. 1990. *Nations and Nationalism since 1780: Programme, Myth, Reality*. Cambridge: Cambridge University Press.

Horkheimer, Max & Theodor W. Adorno. 1947. *Dialektik der Aufklärung* [Dialectic of Enlightenment]. Amsterdam: Querido.

Horton, Richard. 2020. *The Covid-19 Catastrophe: What's Gone Wrong and How to Stop it Happening Again*. Cambridge: Polity.

Jacquet, Jennifer. 2015. *Is Shame Necessary? New Uses for an Old Tool*. London: Penguin Books.

Jaspers, Jürgen. 2018. "Language education policy and sociolinguistics: Toward a new critical engagement." In *The Oxford Handbook of Language Policy and Planning*, edited by James W. Tollefson and Miguel Pérez-Milans, 704–725. Oxford: Oxford University Press.

Jullien, François. 2010. *Le Pont des singes: De la diversité à venir – Fécondité Culturelle face à identité nationale*. Paris: Galilée.

Kendi, Ibram X. 2019. *How to Be an Antiracist*. London: Vintage.

Kerr, Clark. 2001 [1963]. *The Uses of the University*. Cambridge, MA: Harvard University Press.

Kimball, Roger. 1990. *Tenured Radicals: How Politics Has Corrupted Our Higher Education*. Chicago, IL: Ivan R. Dee Publisher.

Klein, Naomi. 2007. *The Shock Doctrine: The Rise of Disaster Capitalism*. London: Penguin Books.

Kutz, Christopher. 2000. *Complicity: Ethics and Law for a Collective Age*. Cambridge: Cambridge University Press.

Le Bras, Hervé. 2017. *L'âge des migrations*. Paris: Éditions Autrement.

Lebor, Adam. 2006. *"Complicity with Evil": The United Nations in the Age of Modern Genocide*. New Haven, CT: Yale University Press.

Leidig, Eviane. 2020. "The far-right is going global." *Foreign Policy*, 21 January 2020, https://foreignpolicy.com/2020/01/21/india-kashmir-modi-eu-hindu-natio nalists-rss-the-far-right-is-going-global/

Lepora, Chiara & Robert E. Goodin. 2013. *On Complicity and Compromise*. Oxford: Oxford University Press.

Lippmann, Walter & Charles Merz. 1920. "A test of the news." *The New Republic* 23 (4 August 1920): 1–42.

Lorenz, Chris. 2012. "'If you're so smart, why are you under surveillance?' Universities, neoliberalism, and New Public Management." *Critical Inquiry* 38(3): 599–629.

Maly, Ico. 2019. "New right metapolitics and the algorithmic activism of Schild & Vrienden." *Social Media + Society*, April-June 2019: 1–15.

Marcuse, Herbert. 1964. *One Dimensional Man*. London: Routledge and Keegan Paul.

Martín Rojo, Luisa & Alfonso Del Percio (eds.). 2019. *Language and Neoliberal Governmentality*. London: Routledge.

McConnell-Ginet, Sally. 2020. *Words Matter: Meaning and Power*. Cambridge: Cambridge University Press.

Mellema, Gregory. 2016. *Complicity and Moral Accountability*. Notre Dame, IN: University of Notre Dame Press.

Mendus, Susan & David Edwards (eds.). 1987. *On Toleration*. Oxford: Oxford University Press.

Monbiot, George. 2016. "Neoliberalism – The ideology at the root of all our problems." *The Guardian*, 15 April 2016.

Mudde, Cas & Cristobal Rovira Kaltwasser. 2017. *Populism: A Very Short Introduction*. Oxford: Oxford University Press.

Müller, Jan-Werner. 2016. *What Is Populism?* Philadelphia, PA: University of Pennsylvania Press.

Murphy, James. 2019. *The Discursive Construction of Blame: The Language of Public Inquiries*. London: Palgrave Macmillan.

Nancy, Jean-Luc. 2010. *Identité: Fragments, Franchises*. Paris: Galilée.

Nemeth, Neil. 2003. *News Ombudsmen in North America: Assessing an Experiment in Social Responsibility*. Santa Barbara, CA: Greenwood Publishing Group.

Newman, John Henry. 1852. *Discourses on the Scope and Nature of University Education* (addressed to the Catholics of Dublin). Dublin: James Duffy.

Nussbaum, Martha. 2010. *Not for Profit: Why Democracy Needs the Humanities*. Princeton, NJ: Princeton University Press.

Östman, Jan-Ola & Anna Solin (eds.). 2016. *Discourse and Responsibility in Professional Settings*. Sheffield: Equinox.

Pariser, Eli. 2011. *The Filter Bubble: What the Internet is Hiding from You*. London: Viking.

Piller, Ingrid. 2016. *Linguistic Diversity and Social Justice: An Introduction to Applied Sociolinguistics*. Oxford: Oxford University Press.

Popper, Karl. 1987. "*Toleration and intellectual responsibility*." In Mendus & Edwards (eds.) (1987), pp. 17–34.

Prins, Baukje. 2002. "The nerve to break taboos: New realism in the Dutch discourse on multiculturalism." *Journal of International Migration and Integration* 3(3/4): 363–379).

Rahier, Jean Muteba. 2003. "Métis/Mulâtre, Mulato, Mulatto, Negro, Moreno, Mundele Kaki, Black: The wanderings and meanderings of identities." In *Problematizing Blackness: Self-Ethnographies by Black Immigrants to the*

United States, edited by Percy Claude Hintzen & Jean Muteba Rahier, pp. 85–112. London: Routledge.

Rampton, Ben & Constadina Charalambous. 2020. "Sociolinguistics and everyday (in)securitization." *Journal of Sociolinguistics* 24: 75–88.

Reich, Charles A. 1970. *The Greening of America*. New York: Bantam Books.

Reif, Linda C. 2004. *The Ombudsman: Good Governance and the International Human Rights System*. Berlin: Springer.

Rosa, Hartmut. 2013. *Alienation and Acceleration: Towards a Critical Theory of Late-Modern Temporality*. Copenhagen: NSU Press & Nordiskt Sommaruniversitet.

Rosovsky, Henry. 1990. *The University: An Owner's Manual*. New York: W.W. Norton & Company.

Saini, Angela. 2019. *Superior: The Return of Race Science*. Boston, MA: Beacon Press.

Scheffer, Paul. 2016. *De vrijheid van de grens* [The freedom of borders]. Amsterdam: De Bezige Bij.

Schiller, Dan. *Objectivity and the News: The Public and the Rise of Commercial Journalism*. Philadelphia, PA: University of Pennsylvania Press.

Schinkel, Willem. 2013. "The imagination of 'society' in measurements of immigrant integration." *Ethnic and Racial Studies* 36(7): 1142–1161.

Schinkel, Willem. 2018. "Against 'immigrant integration': For an end to neocolonial knowledge production." *Comparative Migration Studies* 6:31. doi:10.1186/s40878-018-0095-1

Schneier, Bruce. 2003. *Beyond Fear: Thinking Sensibly about Security in an Uncertain World*. Göttingen: Copernicus Books.

Schudson, Michael. 1978. *Discovering the News: A Social History of American Newspapers*. New York: Basic Books.

Seargeant, Philip & Caroline Tagg. 2019. "Social media and the future of open debate: A user-oriented approach to Facebook's filter bubble conundrum." *Discourse, Context & Media* 27: 41–48.

Selznick, Philip. 1949. *TVA and the Grass Roots: A Study in the Sociology of Formal Organization*. Berkeley, CA: University of California Press.

Sen, Amartya. 1992. *Inequality Reexamined*. Cambridge, MA: Harvard University Press.

Sennett, Richard. 2012. *Together*. New Haven, CT: Yale University Press.

Sieburg, Friedrich. 1933. *Es werde Deutschland*. Frankfurt am Main: Societäts-Verlag (French translation 1933, *Défense du nationalisme allemande*, Paris, Éditions Bernard Grasset).

Silva, Daniel (ed.). 2017. *Language and Violence: Pragmatic Perspectives*. Amsterdam: John Benjamins.

Silverstein, Michael. 2003. *Talking Politics: The Substance of Style from Abe to "W"*. Chicago, IL: Prickly Paradigm Press.

Smith, Anthony D. 2009. *Ethno-Symbolism and Nationalism: A Cultural Approach*. London: Taylor & Francis.

Snyder, Timothy. 2018. *The Road to Unfreedom: Russia, Europe, America*. New York: Tim Duggan Books.

Solnit, Rebecca. 2016. *Hope in the Dark: Untold Histories, Wild Possibilities.* Edinburgh: Canongate Books.

Soros, George. 2019. *In Defence of Open Society.* London: John Murray.

Springer, Simon. 2016. "Fuck neoliberalism." *ACME: An International Journal of Critical Geographies* 15(2): 285–292.

Springer, Simon, Kean Birch & Julie MacLeavy. 2016. "An introduction to neoliberalism." In *The Handbook of Neoliberalism,* edited by S. Springer, K. Birch & J. MacLeavy, pp. 1–14. New York: Routledge.

The Slow Science Academy. 2010. *The Slow Science Manifesto.* http://slow-science. org/slow-science-manifesto.pdf

Thomassen, Bjørn. 2012. "Anthropology and its many modernities: When concepts matter." *Journal of the Royal Anthropological Institute* 18: 160–178.

Thompson, John B. 1990. *Ideology and Modern Culture: Critical Social Theory in the Era of Mass Communication.* Cambridge: Polity Press.

Thompson, John B. 1995. *The Media and Modernity: A Social Theory of the Media.* Stanford, CA: Stanford University Press.

Tomasello, Michael. 1999. *The Cultural Origins of Human Cognition.* Cambridge, MA: Harvard University Press.

Triandafyllidou, Anna, Ruth Wodak & Michał Krzyżanowski (eds.). 2009. *The European Public Sphere and the Media: Europe in Crisis.* New York: Palgrave Macmillan.

Van Parijs, Philippe. 2014. *Linguistic Justice for Europe and for the World.* Oxford: Oxford University Press.

Van Parijs, Philippe & Yannick Vanderborght. 2017. *Basic Income: A Radical Proposal for a Free Society and a Sane Economy.* Cambridge, MA: Harvard University Press.

Verschueren, Jef. 2012. *Ideology in Language Use: Pragmatic Guidelines for Empirical Research.* Cambridge: Cambridge University Press.

Verschueren, Jef, Jan-Ola Östman & Michael Meeuwis (eds.). 2000. *International Communication Monitoring.* Brussels: KVAB.

Vertovec, Steven. 2007. "Super-diversity and its implications." *Ethnic and Racial Studies* 30(6): 1024–1054.

Vertovec, Steven & Susanne Wessendorf (eds.). 2010. *The Multiculturalism Backlash: European Discourses, Policies and Practices.* London: Routledge.

Voltmer, Katrin. 2013. *The Media in Transitional Democracies.* Cambridge: Polity Press.

Vygotsky, L.S. 1978. *Mind in Society: The Development of Higher Psychological Processes.* Cambridge, MA: Harvard University Press.

Wagner, Peter. 2012. *Modernity: Understanding the Present.* Cambridge: Polity Press.

Watson, Rod & Jeff Coulter. 2008. "The debate over cognitivism." *Theory, Culture & Society* 25(2): 1–17.

Weber, Max. 1922. *Wirtschaft und Gesellschaft.* Tübingen: Mohr.

Wicker, Tom. 1975. *On Press.* New York: Berkley Publishing Corporation.

Wieviorka, Michel. 2020. *Pour une démocratie de combat.* Paris: Robert Laffont.

Wilkinson, Richard & Kate Pickett. 2009. *The Spirit Level: Why Equality is Better for Everyone*. London: Penguin Books.

Wilson, Robin & Thomas Hennessey. 1997. *With All Due Respect: Pluralism and Parity of Esteem*. Belfast: Democratic Dialogue.

Wolff, Richard D. 2021. *The Sickness is the System: When Capitalism Fails to Save Us from Pandemics or Itself*. New York: Democracy at Work.

Zienkowski, Jan & Benjamin De Cleen. 2017. "De-legitimizing labour unions: On the metapolitical fantasies that inform discourse on striking terrorists, blackmailing the government and taking hard-working citizen hostage." *Tilburg Papers in Cultural Studies* 176.

Zinn, Howard. 2011. *On Race*. (Introduction by Cornell West.) New York: Seven Stories Press.

Zúquete, José Pedro. 2018. *The Identitarians: The Movement against Globalism and Islam in Europe*. Notre Dame, IN: Notre Dame University Press.

Zweig, Stefan. 1944. *Die Welt von gestern* [The world of yesterday]. Zug, Switzerland: Williams Verlag.

Index